The Credibility Code

Published by Meritus Books
info@meritusbooks.com

Library of Congress Control Number: 2012906993

To buy this book in quantity or schedule a speaking engagement, contact the author.

Email: info@thecredibilitycode.com
Website: www.thecredibilitycode.com

Cover design by Andy Rado
Interior design by Leslie Waltzer, Crowfoot Design

Printed in the United States of America
First edition: May 2012

CARA HALE ALTER

The Credibility Code

How to project confidence & competence
when it matters most

To my purest source of joy – Ed, Nick, and Cassie

Contents

Foreword

As a leader in global health, I know that the right medicine is useless without the ability to deliver it to those who need it. The same is true for ideas. Credibility is not about having great ideas but, rather, about saying those ideas so that people will listen.

It took me a while to figure this out. I used to think technical expertise was the most important ingredient for success until half the audience fell asleep during my first lecture. Then Cara Hale Alter gave me the tools to connect my ideas to people. Individually, these skills seemed deceptively simple: hands in the gesture box, level 4 volume, nose and eyes in alignment. Together, they have become the most powerful tools of my career.

Suddenly people started to listen more carefully. I engaged their full attention. They began to ask nuanced questions. They wanted more. I was invited to speak to larger and larger groups. My reach went from local to national to global. My ideas hadn't changed; instead, I was delivering them much more effectively.

I am blessed with brilliant, dedicated, and tenacious students who are improving people's health around the world. My students are overflowing with ideas, energy, and idealism. But I tell every student, "Ideas go nowhere if people don't hear you. If you really want to have an impact, learn Cara's code!"

In these pages, you'll find a step-by-step methodology for building credibility one communication skill at a time. Consider it a toolbox. Carry it with you. Mark it up. Do the exercises. Go on the field trips. It will be the most important investment of your career. It was for me.

David R. Bangsberg, MD, MSc, MPH
Director of the Massachusetts General Hospital
Center for Global Health
Associate Professor, Harvard Medical School

Introduction

Credibility. Personal power. Executive presence. These are not elusive qualities that some people have and some don't: Specific behaviors trigger these assessments. This book takes an in-depth look at what these behaviors are, how much impact they have on others, and how much control you have over them.

In today's business world, being credible is not enough. You have to *look* credible. It must be observable in all of your face-to-face communications. Many people, however, no matter how passionate and talented, can not move forward in their careers because their credibility is not immediately apparent.

Here's what I assume: You are smart, capable, and competent. And I'm sure you want others to immediately recognize this about you. If you want to show people your potential, stand out in a sea of applicants, win that contract, or get that promotion, you'll have to convince others of your abilities.

It's possible that your credentials alone can serve that need; having an extensive resume or a string of letters after your name is very helpful. But if your qualifications on paper aren't enough to assure your status, you'll have to *project* the credibility you deserve.

The Credibility Code makes the quality of credibility tangible and actionable. It lays out the ground rules, the explicit *codes of conduct* for looking confident, capable, and credible. By better understanding which specific behaviors raise or lower your status in the eyes of people around you, you can take charge of your own image.

Who can gain by reading this book?

Whether you're meeting one-on-one with a client, interacting with colleagues around the conference table, broadcasting on YouTube, or delivering a formal presentation to a packed audience, gaining control over the image you project will give you a substantial edge. It doesn't matter if you're a top executive with decades of experience or a graduate fresh out of college. By helping you understand how your visual and auditory cues are being perceived, *The Credibility Code* gives you leverage— leverage that can open doors and open minds; leverage that can change fixed opinions and strengthen new ones; leverage that can, ultimately, determine the direction and success of your career.

Split-second assessments

Nalini Ambady, a social psychologist and leading expert in nonverbal communication, coined the term "thin slicing." It's the ability to observe patterns based on only a thin slice of experience. In one revealing experiment, Ambady showed college students video clips of teachers and asked them to choose adjectives to describe the teachers. Initially she showed the students 30 seconds of video. They had no problem forming quick assessments. But with subsequent groups of students, she cut the clips down incrementally until the clips were only two seconds long. Not only were the assessments remarkably consistent regardless of the length of the clips, the evaluations were very similar to those of the students who sat through an entire semester in the instructor's class.

People make up their minds about us at lightning speed, without taking the time to analyze why they find us likable, authoritative, confident . . . or "insert-adjective-here." Their conclusions are based on observable cues, nonverbal signals such as the position of our chin, the width of our stance, the speed of our gestures, or the duration of our eye contact. Together these components form a composite that defines the perceptions others have of us.

While the study above is remarkable because it shows how quickly this happens, even more astounding is the fact that there is *consistency*. When we watch a video of a stranger, we all use roughly the same adjectives to describe that person. If this is possible, some kind of ground rules must be governing our observations.

Many people believe that credibility, like beauty, is in the eye of the beholder. In truth, very specific behaviors lead us to an assessment of credibility. In the next eight chapters, I'll lay out explicitly what these behaviors are.

The ground rules are not as deeply hidden as you may think. Pay attention to the metaphors in your language, and you'll find your action plan right in front of you. If you'd like people to describe you as having a strong spine and a level head, you must literally have a strong spine and a level head! If you'd like to be a powerful voice in your community, you must literally possess a powerful voice.

While this book will delve deeply into nonverbal communication, it won't teach you how to tell if someone is lying or how to flirt at a party. My objective is much more specific: To focus exclusively on those behaviors that affect your credibility in face-to-face interactions. Once you understand the ground rules, you'll discover your image is within your control.

A little advice

In my early days, I worked as the receptionist at a prominent law firm. When I confessed to the senior partner that I often felt intimidated by the high-powered executives who daily approached my desk, he gave me a bit of advice that has stuck with me. "There's no real trick to looking confident," he said. "Just be yourself and don't do anything distracting."

That's simultaneously the best and the worst advice I've ever received. I agree with it wholeheartedly, and I've spent my career trying to figure out how to pull it off! If you can "just be yourself" in the middle of a high-stakes meeting—when adrenaline is flowing, you're being hammered by challenging questions, your thinking is growing fuzzy, and several voices in your head are screaming instructions—congratulations!

For most people, however, when the pressure is on, being yourself is like a roulette game. You don't know which version of you is going to show up—the intelligent, capable human being you know yourself to be or some lesser version of you.

The paradox: The more *self*-conscious we are, the more difficult it is to be ourselves. And we can be distinctly different people in different situations. I've talked to countless people who say to me, "I'm fine one-on-one, but as soon as I get in front of a group, I fall apart." Or, "I'm perfectly competent when I'm with my team, but when I have to meet with the senior executives, I can't think straight."

This book isn't about coming across at your best during *perfect* conditions. It's about being at your best under *any* conditions. To get there, you'll need an in-depth understanding of what your best self looks like.

And this brings me to the second half of the senior partner's advice, "Don't do anything distracting." Here's another paradox: Our distracting behaviors aren't distracting to us. We are oblivious to them because no one does distracting behaviors on purpose.

Let's face it: We're all trying our best. If we're ineffective, it is almost certainly *unintentional*. We are either unaware of the behavior we're exhibiting or unaware of the impact it's having on others.

We start by swallowing a bitter pill: If others aren't seeing us the way we see ourselves and if they aren't recognizing our talents, it is almost certainly something *we* are doing. This doesn't sound like good news, but it is, because the more you understand how you contribute to the problem, the more power you have to fix it.

Accidental messages

People are frequently unaware of how they come across. And here are just a few examples of how accidental signals can cause a divide between how we see ourselves and how others perceive us.

- Isabella described herself as extremely timid, so she was dismayed to discover her new coworkers perceived her as hostile and judgmental. When she felt uncomfortable, her unconscious defense mechanism was to retreat. Her posture became rigid, and she shut down all facial reactions. Ironically, what felt to Isabella like "deer in the headlights" panic looked to her coworkers like a cold, aggressive stare.

- Grant felt ready to take on more of a leadership role in his division, but he was disappointed when he was consistently passed over for promotion. He was unaware that his speech pattern was overloaded with filler words. He would often say "uh" or "um" four or five times per sentence. Internally, he felt confident, but externally he sounded perpetually tentative and distracted.

- Janelle thought of herself as friendly and passionate but confessed that others often described her as aggressive and pushy. She was totally unaware of how her hands punctuated each phrase with sharp, emphatic gestures whenever she spoke. The harder she tried to make a connection, the sharper her gestures became. She was virtually pushing people away.

- Because Pascal was uncomfortable presenting in front of his colleagues, he thrust his hands deep within his pockets. But he couldn't keep his hands still and, unbeknownst to Pascal, his hands continued to gesture throughout his presentation. Everyone found his talk very entertaining, but not in the way Pascal had intended.

The camera doesn't lie

Have you ever seen a videotape of how you walk? Others can recognize you from behind or at a distance because of *your unique stride and gait*. However, very few of us are able to recognize ourselves without more distinctive clues. We rarely get an outside view of how we move through the world.

My workshops rely heavily on the video camera to capture how we look. Most people are amazed at what they see. Nearly all of us have unintentional signals derailing our effectiveness—a bobbing head, the tendency to fidget, asymmetrical posture, weak volume, too many filler words—the list is extensive.

We all carry habits acquired from years of communicating: Some are good; others are less so. Just as junk can pile up in that proverbial kitchen drawer, extraneous signals can creep into our style.

It makes sense that we're relatively unaware of our own mannerisms since there is no way we can actively focus on the hundreds of signals we are exhibiting at once—posture, gestures, volume, pitch, pace, articulation, inflection, eye contact, head movement, and so on. In order to focus on higher-level communication skills, such as forming words into sentences and interpreting reactions, we lock these lower-level behaviors into our muscle memory, our subroutines, so that they run on automatic pilot.

And thank goodness for the genius of the human brain that makes subroutines a part of our process. Driving, typing, dancing, and reading are all possible because we have the ability to group precise individual steps into fluid subroutines.

But understanding subroutines also helps us understand why we have unintentional behaviors in our style. Once a bad habit creeps into a subroutine, we pay no attention to it. It becomes embedded in the program. This is why smart, capable people can be oblivious to their own bad habits.

The four stages of competency

In order to transform a bad habit into a good one, you'll need to travel through the "Four Stages of Competency." This learning theory states that when learning or acquiring any new skill, we start out "unconsciously incompetent." Essentially, we don't know that we don't know. At this stage, not only does the individual *not* know how to do the behavior but he or she is blind to the deficit. In the learning process, we become "consciously incompetent." We now know that we don't know it. Frankly, this is a very difficult place to be: No one enjoys being consciously incompetent. However, depending on how painful this realization is determines how quickly we move into stage three: "consciously competent." When we focus on the behavior, we can do it. We are proficient, but it takes effort. As we continue to practice this new behavior, we ultimately become "unconsciously competent." We no longer have to focus on the behavior to do it well. It has now become a new subroutine.

As you move through the chapters of this book, you may find yourself moving through these four stages of learning.

Unconsciously incompetent

Consciously incompetent

Consciously competent

Unconsciously competent

Taking control

The first step to taking control of your image is to identify the exact behaviors that are influencing your appearance of credibility. In chapters 1 through 4, we'll look at the explicit *codes of conduct* for posture, gestures, vocal skills, and eye contact. Adopt these essential behaviors, and you'll be well on your way to projecting credibility.

In chapter 5, we'll take a look at what *not* to do. "Derailers" are the distracting behaviors that are almost always invisible to us but undercut our credibility with others. Our blind spots often have the biggest impact on our image.

While looking credible is a wonderful baseline, truly effective communication is an interaction *between* people. It's not enough for you to look good; you need to make a connection with your listener. To truly raise the bar on your communication skills, shift your focus from yourself to *them*. In chapter 6, we'll address the skills of connection: projection, eliciting a response, and attentive listening.

Communication styles run a spectrum from being authoritative to being approachable. Exceptional communicators know how to project both qualities at the same time, and in chapter 7, we discuss the perfect balance. If you need to bolster your image on either end of the spectrum, I identify specific behaviors that send the right messages.

Finally, in chapter 8, we tackle how to keep your progress moving forward including the importance of videotaped feedback, steps for self-evaluation, and how to put an action plan in place.

> *At the end of each chapter, you'll find links to short videos demonstrating the skills just covered.*

At the end of each chapter, you'll find links to short videos demonstrating the skills just covered. Depending on your learning style, you can watch the videos before or after you read each chapter.

Each step of the way includes case studies, practice exercises, and "field trips" to help you develop your skills right away. Practice exercises are drills to do in the privacy of your home or office. Field trips are an invitation to get up from your chair or desk, head out into the world, and test what you've learned.

Start by learning which behaviors build credibility and which don't. Examine your personal style and meticulously weed out the behaviors that don't serve you. Finally, practice until your new behaviors become so habitual that they'll stick with you even under pressure.

A note about your script

While most of this book discusses the power of your behaviors, I don't want to give the impression that your words aren't important. Your content, the actual script of what you say, is vital. It's the very reason you are having the converstaion to begin with.

Before listeners can hear *what* you have to say, however, they need to create a filter through which they listen to you. They decide *where to put* what you have to say. Does it go in the box that says, "Yes! Act on this right away," or the box that says, "Hmm. I'll have to think that over . . ."? Your image determines where they log the information you give them.

When time is short and personal resources are low, most people spend their energy working on their script and ignore their skills. I encourage you to reverse that trend. Once your skills are strongly embedded in your subroutines, they'll be there when you need them. The script, however, will change with every conversation.

You might argue that the more you know your script, the more you can concentrate on your skills—stance, gestures, voice, and eye contact —and that's true, to a point. Imagine it the other way around: Develop your skills. Work on them until they are habits. Then the *only* thing you have to concentrate on is what you have to say. Wouldn't that put you more at ease?

Play along with me for a moment: Let's say you have to deliver a message you are extremely familiar with—material you know forward and backward. Now pretend I ask you to deliver this information while ice-skating. If you don't know how to ice skate already, do you think you'll be able to move forward on the ice and say your message out loud at the same time? Unlikely. When struggling with a new physical task, verbal processing is the first thing to go out the window. But if you know how to ice-skate, can you deliver your message and skate at the same time? Of course. Ice-skating is a "subroutine." It will be as easy as walking and talking at the same time.

I'm sure you've experienced going blank under pressure. You've adequately prepared for a high-stakes conversation, but in the midst of it you completely lose your train of thought. Mortified, you promise yourself, "Next time, I'll know my material even better." Unfortunately you're focusing on the wrong subroutine.

By cementing these physical skills into your muscle memory, you free up your verbal processing. Invest time into creating good habits, and all of your communication becomes easier.

A postscript on our worldly communications

With very few exceptions, the signals discussed in this book are human, not cultural, interpretations—how human beings assess other human beings. However, to what degree certain behaviors are valued can vary widely from culture to culture. For example, keeping your head level (as opposed to dipping your chin down or tilting your head) is viewed as confidence in all cultures. But some cultures more highly value showing deference when speaking. In these cultures, holding the head level, while confident, could be taken as a sign of disrespect.

Being warm and friendly, even subservient, in some cultures, can be a far better way to do business than being authoritative or assertive. To be effective, it's important to understand the values of the people with whom you interact. To that end, this book will focus on qualities that are valued in a Western business culture. While I may point out areas of extreme cultural differences (such as eye contact or hand gestures), it should be assumed that my perspective is from a Western point of view.

*To watch a short video of the author
demonstrating the skills in this chapter,
scan the box above or
enter this URL into your browser.*

www.thecredibilitycode.com/video/ixrv34

CHAPTER 1

Posture:
Taking a Stand

*"Your playing small does not serve the world.
There is nothing enlightened about shrinking so that
other people won't feel insecure around you.
We are all meant to shine."*

– MARIANNE WILLIAMSON

Cesar Millan is remarkably gifted with dogs. He takes dogs that other trainers have given up on—extremely aggressive dogs, dogs with destructive habits or unusual phobias—and in a short period of time persuades them to behave in more socially acceptable ways. If you've ever seen an episode of *The Dog Whisperer*, you've seen how skillfully he uses his body language to establish his status.

In one episode, Cesar visited a family with an especially vicious dog. The dog was extremely protective of the backyard, making it treacherous for people outside of the family to enter the area. The family was concerned they would have to euthanize the dog, and Cesar was their last hope.

After gathering the facts from the family in the living room, Cesar headed for the backyard where the dog was waiting. The family adamantly exclaimed, "Have you not been listening! Don't go out there. He'll kill you!" Cesar was undeterred. While the family and the cameraman watched through the sliding glass door, Cesar, relaxed but purposeful, stepped into the backyard. The dog did not attack. Cesar moved around the backyard for about 10 minutes. The dog watched, more curious than threatened. Finally Cesar approached the dog, gracefully attached a leash to his collar, and took him out through the gate for a walk.

In the dog world, Cesar Milan has exceptional leadership presence. Dogs immediately recognize his status as alpha dog. They aren't responding to magical vibes; they recognize his leadership by the way he carries himself.

Cesar walks tall with his head level. At the same time, his movements are fluid and unrestricted. He is attentive and deliberate, yet relaxed. This combination of strength and fluidity helps him project authority without appearing threatening. And these same body language signals work equally well in human-to-human communication. Let me relay a true story from one of my clients to help bring this message to the work world.

The CEO who didn't get the new job

The stakes were high in the search for the new chief executive officer of an architectural firm. Headhunters had reviewed and forwarded the résumés of several candidates to oversee the 200-person company. Five highly qualified candidates were selected for interviews.

After a first round of phone interviews, one candidate stood out. He sounded confident over the phone. Good track record. Excellent experience. The management search committee sensed he was the one and flew him out for an interview.

The interview went smoothly; the candidate seemed to fit the bill. Yet, after the candidate left, each member of the search committee voted against hiring him. When they discussed the reasons, they all realized it came down to one moment: At one point during the interview, the candidate stood up and walked to the counter to refill his coffee. His slumped posture and weak spine made him look tired and worn out, and, in that moment, each member of the search committee concluded he was not the energized, engaged CEO who they wanted to lead their company.

You would never think something as superficial as bad posture could cost you a job, yet I heard this story directly from the search committee (as I was training their new CEO).

Posture Codes of Conduct
- Keep your spine tall and strong.
- Stand with your weight balanced equally over both feet.
- Keep your head level.
- Point your nose directly at the listener.
- Command the space around you.

POSTURE CODE #1
Keep your spine tall and strong

Strong posture—keeping your spine strong and vertical—brings added credibility to everything you say and do. You'll look more dynamic, more focused, and more purposeful. Such an image comes in handy in all situations, from standing out at a cocktail party, to getting what you want in the boardroom, to showing someone on the subway that you're not a person to mess with.

Follow the metaphor

The guidelines for appearing credible and confident can be found in the metaphors of everyday language. Would you like to be described as . . . ?

Stable	On solid footing	Standing on your own two feet
Grounded	Having a strong spine	Being a pillar of strength
Balanced	Having a firm backbone	Not easily pushed over
Straightforward	Being levelheaded	Head square on your shoulders
Upright	Taking a firm stand	Standing your ground

Now compare those words and phrases to being described as a slouch, off-balance, unstable, lacking a backbone, or shifty.

POSTURE CODE #2

Stand with your weight balanced equally over both feet

There is a big difference separating what *feels* comfortable and what *looks* comfortable. When under stress, we often default to behaviors that feel good, even if they don't represent us well. The most common defense mechanism for managing intimidating situations is to act casual and to make ourselves look smaller.

When the pressure is on during a job interview or an important proposal, for example, most of us try to mask our discomfort by taking on a more casual stance. Our posture goes from balanced to asymmetrical. We stand leaning into a hip, shoulders on an angle, head tilted. We may even cross one leg in front of the other. If the goal is to look nonthreatening, such actions might work to our advantage. But while this posture definitely looks casual, we give up the opportunity to look self-assured and in control.

It's important to ask yourself which characteristic you really want to project: Do you want to look more casual . . . or more *comfortable?* People who look comfortable stand tall with their weight evenly balanced over both feet. Their posture seems to say, "I've got the situation completely under control."

When we feel intimidated, most of us will pull in and take up less space; we subtly make ourselves smaller so as to be less of a target. We may do this by placing our feet close together, tucking our arms tightly to our sides, and restricting our movement to a very small bubble around us. But to look comfortable and confident, strengthen your spine, open up, and move freely. In short, command the space around you.

Practice exercise: Stand up for yourself

Take a moment to test optimal standing posture. Stand with your weight balanced equally over both feet. Because men and women have a different center of gravity, men should align their feet directly under their shoulder joints, and women should align their feet directly under their hip joints. Lengthen your spine so you are as tall as you can be without feeling stiff. Elongate your neck so that your chin is level.

While keeping your trunk stable, add hand gestures and head movement. Make sure your elbows aren't pinned to your sides or held out in space. Try not to let your shoulders reverberate with the movements of your hands. When looking around the room, avoid twisting at the waist. Your head should move like a camera on a tripod, enabling you to pan easily around the room while your base stays still.

Your spine and shoulders should form a *T*, straight and strong. Think of this as the scaffolding for the rest of your body. Your head, arms, and feet can move freely, but the *T* always stays strong. Check out your posture in front of a full-length mirror.

Take a field trip around the office

Develop the habit of practicing in everyday moments. You can start by taking a quick walk around your office. Your intention is to have short conversations with several colleagues. While standing at each colleague's cubicle, balance your weight equally over both feet. Head to the kitchen and stand in optimal posture while you glance at the contents of the vending machine. If you bump into some co-workers in the hallway, chat with them for a moment, all the while being attentive to your posture. Even when *they* are talking, keep your weight balanced and spine straight.

You can find hundreds of opportunities to practice optimal posture throughout the day—ordering your coffee at the coffee bar, waiting in line at the grocery store, even commuting in your car. Don't save your excellent posture for "important" situations. *Make it habitual.* Once it is, your posture will exhibit confidence and purpose everywhere you go.

Establish your place at the conference table

Most of us spend a good deal of our working lives sitting down, so pull up a chair and think about how to look confident around the conference room table or across the desk.

The same rules apply to establishing credibility in a seated position as when standing: keep your spine strong, hold your shoulders level, and own the space around you. Try to keep your tailbone against the back of the chair so your lumbar is supported and you look as tall as possible. If you allow your tailbone to scoot forward, even an inch, your posture rounds and your status deflates. Don't slouch!

Sometimes the chair itself can be a problem since many office chairs have a deep seat built to accommodate the average male thighbone. If you are shorter than average and sit all the way back, your feet might not touch the floor, making you feel like a little kid at the grown-up table. You don't want to lower your chair because your height at the table also affects your status. So what can you do?

Your best option may be to sit on the edge of your seat. This is also a good tactic if your office furniture is so casual that you could be swallowed up by a puffy chair or couch. This position may not be as comfortable as leaning back, but you'll maintain your presence in the room.

If you're sitting at a table, set your briefcase or bag on the floor to prop up your feet. This may sound extreme, but I know executives who have special boxes at their feet so they can raise their chairs to be the tallest person in the room without their feet dangling.

It's tempting to sit close to the table and prop your elbows on it, but you'll look more authoritative by giving yourself a little space. Don't let the proximity of the table trap you into being small. Keep your torso about six to eight inches *away from the table*. Doing so enables you to own the space in front of you and frees your hands to become involved in the conversation. I'll go into more detail about this in the next chapter, but note that interactive gestures not only will help you be more engaging but they will help you create a stronger relationship with your listeners.

POSTURE CODE #3
Keep your head level

One of the key behaviors that signals personal power is being level-headed—literally the ability to keep your head level when speaking. The power of this one skill can be transforming.

The position of your chin sends a big message. If you consistently hold your chin a little too high, you are likely to be viewed as cocky, condescending, or even aggressive. You could be described as "looking down on someone" or "having your nose in the air." On the other hand, if you consistently dip your chin, you are likely to be viewed as shy or submissive. We often encourage someone who looks deflated by saying, "Hey, chin up!"

And avoid head tilting since it can imply you are questioning yourself, looking for approval, or softening the force of your words. The goal is to be levelheaded both literally and figuratively.

To send a message of confidence, move your head independently of your shoulders: Again, the *T* of your spine and shoulders stays still while your head, like a camera on a tripod, can pan easily around the room.

The same rules apply when you are seated in a chair: Rather than swiveling as you look from one person to another, keep your body position still and let your head move independently.

One of the key behaviors that signals personal power is being level-headed—literally the ability to keep your head level when speaking. The power of this one skill can be transforming.

Practice exercise: Level out

Take a moment right now to observe the space around you. Start by lengthening your spine and leveling your head. Moving only your head, scan your environment and make sure your torso stays still. Stillness is a high-status, authoritative behavior. Achieving it means no twisting in the direction you are looking. The more you practice this, the more you will feel an inner sense of power.

Speakers who keep their shoulders still while gazing around the room exhibit poise and authority. Think of how eagles and owls survey their surroundings: Their heads move fluidly while their bodies remain still. Typically, we describe them as regal and wise. Compare these descriptors to how differently we refer to those birds that twitter and tilt their heads all the time.

POSTURE CODE #4

Point your nose directly at the listener

It's important to keep your spine strong and to look around the room with a level head. But to perfect your posture, one more body part needs attention—your nose. To convey yourself as straightforward and focused, make sure your nose points directly toward the person you are addressing. As you look around the room, wherever you eyes land, your nose should be pointing there as well.

Try this quick exercise: Keep your nose pointed toward this page while you let your eyes look around the room independently for a few seconds. Imagine how your behavior might look from the outside. When your eyes move independently from your nose, you can look sneaky, scared, shy, nervous, judgmental, or skeptical. Have you heard the phrase "looking out the corner of your eye at someone"? To avoid giving off negative signals, make sure your nose points directly at the person you are looking at.

Practice exercise: Get face to face

At your next meeting, imagine that you have a laser pointer attached to the end of your nose. As you look around the room while speaking or listening, ask yourself if the laser pointer's red dot would be landing directly on the face of each person you engage. If so, you know you are effectively face-to-face.

POSTURE CODE #5
Command the space around you

Having strong posture and the ability to move your head and arms freely is important in any conversation, whether you are seated or standing, or before an audience of one or many. But if you are giving a formal presentation at the front of the room, the bar is raised another notch. Now you must also *take command of the room.*

Moving fluidly at the front of the room can help you to look comfortable and in charge. But make note here that learning how to stand still is the higher priority. Only when you can effortlessly stand still, feet grounded and weight balanced, should you give yourself permission to move around.

The most common mistake people make when at the front of the room is moving too often and never coming to stillness. There are many negative terms we might use to describe this behavior: wandering, shifting, repositioning, dancing, or being unfocused. To look grounded and stable, remember the following rules:

1. Wherever you move, stand still when you get there. Watching someone in a perpetual state of motion can be distracting and tiring.
2. Move no more than once every paragraph or so. That's about every 45 to 60 seconds. Let your subject matter be your guide: When you move to a new idea in your presentation, feel free to move to a new location.

3. Keep your posture open to the entire group. If you move to a new place in the room, you may need to readjust your angle so that your torso is open to everyone.

4. Finally, keep your head up while you're moving. An inexperienced speaker will often look down when walking. By maintaining eye contact with your audience, you will have much more credibility than someone who appears to be having a conversation with the floor.

When to pitch your points . . . and when to listen

When you are delivering a message, the preceding guidelines can help you win over your audience. But if you're the one listening, relax the rules—and your spine. It's important to acknowledge the difference between speaking posture and listening posture. When you're listening, feel free to round your spine so you look like a good receiver.

Picture a baseball game; specifically, imagine a pitcher and a catcher: Each one adopts a body position suited for the job at hand. The same idea is relevant when talking and listening. If you're talking, you're the pitcher. You need a strong spine, a level head, and the energy to throw your message. If you're the listener, you're the catcher. You want to look receptive by rounding your spine and relaxing into your chair. Even simply tilting your head can indicate you are receptive and open.

Watch out, however, for the problem of slipping into speaking mode but staying in listening posture. This could be the culprit if you feel you're not being heard in meetings. For example, has this ever happened to you? You make a suggestion, but nobody responds. Then five minutes later a colleague makes the same suggestion and gets rewarded with a chorus of "Good idea!"

> *If you're not getting the attention and credit you deserve, ask yourself if your body language is responsible; maybe it's sending the message of a catcher rather than a pitcher.*

If you're not getting the attention and credit you deserve, ask yourself if your body language is responsible; maybe it's sending the message of a catcher rather than a pitcher. Adjust your posture to send the physical signal that you're ready to take the spotlight.

Take a field trip to the gym

Good posture sends a message of strength because it actually takes *strength*! Standing tall and balanced takes muscle power. Develop the stamina to turn great posture into a solid habit through weight training, yoga, or Pilates. The time you invest will be well worth the effort.

Moving on

The posture codes of conduct above will help you send the message that you are a pillar of strength and a force to be reckoned with. But that's only part of what your body language can do. If you'd like to be seen as engaging and interactive, get your hand and facial gestures involved. Your posture creates solidity; your gestures create fluidity.

Your hands give off subtle information about your personality and comfort level. Have you played poker lately? What are the "tells" of your speaking persona?

*To watch a short video of the author
demonstrating the skills in this chapter,
scan the box above or
enter this URL into your browser.*

www.thecredibilitycode.com/video/pmqd88

CHAPTER 2

Gestures:
Reaching Out

*"When watching adults as a child, I remember strongly
that what was coming out of their mouths was one thing,
but the way that they were holding their bodies
and moving was usually the real thing."*
– ALONZO KING, CHOREOGRAPHER

In poker parlance, a "tell" is a subtle nonverbal signal that reveals information about the apparent strength or weakness of your hand. The most common poker tells are "acting" tells—acting confident when you're bluffing or looking forlorn when you're holding a winner. For the professional poker player, *subconscious tells* are the most revealing. Unlike what we see in the movies, this is rarely an inadvertent scratch of the ear or an absentminded pull on the shirtsleeve. Subconscious tells involve human emotions and behaviors that are difficult to control. Professional players scrutinize subtle shifts in their opponents' breathing, posture, facial tension, and eye contact, looking for signs of excitement or disappointment. They glean information about opponents' decision-making processes by noticing how long they study their cards, if they rearrange them, how quickly they reach for the new card, or whether they glance at their chips.

One of the richest moments for reading tells is the moment the cards are first dealt. Inexperienced players look at their cards right away, but the expert player does not. The expert will take that moment to observe how the others react to their cards.

Similarly, in important face-to-face conversations, the first few moments are quite revealing. Abundant clues about someone's level of comfort come from watching his or her hands. If the hands are still, stiff, gripping, fumbling, or fidgeting while he or she is speaking, these silent signals almost always indicate some discomfort with the situation. Hands that are relaxed and fluidly engaged are a sign of being at ease.

I've witnessed the following scene so often that I could safely bet money on the probability of the result. The presenter steps to the front of the room, positions himself with his hands clasped in front of him—in the "fig leaf" position—and several sentences go by with no movement of the hands. Then one natural gesture pops into the conversation, and the hands go back to the fig leaf. Another gesture pops into the conversation; soon the presenter's hands break free of their invisible restraints and take on a life of their own, fully engaged in the conversation. This is the moment when the speaker looks as if he's finally warmed up. The whole process typically takes from 30 seconds to a minute.

Gesture Codes of Conduct
- Avoid "masking" your face and hands.
- Engage your words and hands simultaneously.
- Reach out to your listener.
- Keep your hands in the gesture box.

A show of hands

Hand gesturing is part of our communication process; it's how we grapple with our words and massage our ideas. When we are feeling perfectly comfortable, our hands move easily from one natural gesture to the next. This is not a culturally specific behavior; it's hardwired into all of us throughout the world. Even blind people gesture when they speak.

Even blind people gesture when they speak. It's not something we learn visually but is a form of communication much deeper and older than the spoken word.

It's not something we learn visually but is a form of communication much deeper and older than the spoken word.

What's unusual about hand gesturing is that it's an *unconscious* communication behavior. Even though we are not thinking about our hands, they participate actively in the conversation. We're not aware of them until we become *self*-conscious, and then we don't know what to do with our hands. They become awkward appendages attached to the ends of our arms.

The most common question I hear in my workshops is "What should I do with my hands?" The answer: Just do what you normally do. But therein lies the problem: *Because gesturing is an unconscious behavior, we don't know what we normally do.* Even thinking about our hands seems unnatural.

This lack of awareness leads some people to believe they don't talk with their hands. Many times people have said to me, "I know you say everyone gestures, but I don't." And as they say this, they'll point to themselves and shrug their shoulders.

If you don't talk with your hands, you are a rare human being. And it wouldn't be accidental: You would have spent an inordinate amount of time training it out of your system because hand gestures are an innate part of our conversation.

The winning combination is body posture that is still and solid—like a pillar of strength—with hand and facial gestures that are interactive and expressive.

GESTURE CODE #1
Avoid masking your face and hands

Here's the good news and the bad news: You don't have to learn how to gesture—you do it hundreds of times throughout the day. But you do need to learn how to handle those moments when you become self-conscious of your gestures. The key isn't learning how to gesture; it's learning not to "mask" your gestures.

When we feel uncomfortable or on the spot, nearly all of us go into some sort of masking behavior to hide our discomfort. It can take the form of clasped hands, crossed arms, hands in pockets, or a "poker face." The defining characteristic of masking is a lack of fluidity of the hands or the face. We rarely mask intentionally. It just subtly creeps into our style. The result, however, is that we are likely to appear stiff or nervous.

In the last chapter, we learned that stillness is a good thing. But fluidity is also a good thing. Animating your style can help you look engaged and dynamic. The issue is using the right type of animation. And the winning combination is body posture that is still and solid—like a pillar of strength—with hand and facial gestures that are interactive and expressive.

Masking positions to avoid

Let's start by taking a look at what *not* to do. Here are the most common "tells" people use to manage their hands when they feel self-conscious.

- **Arms crossed.** This includes the full version with arms crossed tightly across the chest and the more subtle variation with one arm hanging by the side while the other crosses over to hold the elbow.
- **Hands in pockets.** This makes the awkwardness truly disappear—no hands at all.
- **Thumbs hooked in pockets or waistband.** While this might seem like a non-threatening gesture, it can look too casual and disengaged.

- **Fig leaf.** Your hands are clasped in front of your body, right where Adam's hands would be if he didn't have a fig leaf to preserve his modesty.
- **Military position.** Your hands are clasped behind your back. Picture a stoic-looking general, and you'll see why this stance is not very personable.
- **Hand gripping.** Your fingers are tightly intertwined, or you have one hand clasped over the other. (*Loosely* resting your hands together is not a problem; it's the white knuckles you want to avoid.)
- **Spider on the mirror.** In this position, all the fingertips of one hand touch all the fingertips of the other hand. If you've ever seen a bad actor trying to look pensive, you'll recognize this gesture.
- **Steeple position.** With this position, similar to the one above, the index fingers form a steeple while the other fingers intertwine.
- **Self-touch.** This includes nervously playing with your rings or touching your face, clothing, or hair.

"Self-touch" is a behavioral psychology term for something we all do under stress. If I am suddenly shocked by a bit of news, my hand might fly up to my face to cover my mouth. Or, if I begin to worry, I might wring my hands together. In times of great stress, we might literally wrap our arms around our bodies and hold on.

Signals of self-touch are rampant when someone is uncomfortable. One might hold on to a finger, a button, or a coat hem. I recently video-taped a banking vice president who held onto the thumb of her left hand with the finger tips of her right hand throughout her 10-minute presentation. Without the proof of my video camera, she never would have believed she had done it!

Because these masking positions are so common, listeners expect this kind of behavior at the beginning of a meeting or presentation. The lesson is clear for you: If you do not exhibit these behaviors, you can positively differentiate yourself from those who do.

The school board candidate

A colleague told me an embarrassing story about the speeches she heard at a school board candidates' night. The first six candidates presented themselves in a range from stiff to formal to folksy. Then came candidate seven.

He was a good-hearted person who ran a shelter for runaway teens. But he finished nearly every statement by nervously tucking his shirt into his pants. Seven times his hands disappeared—*deep into his pants, front and back.* It wasn't intentional; he was not conscious of doing it. But as you might imagine, when the votes were tallied, candidate seven came in last. The lesson: Tighten your belt.

Polite but guarded

Picture someone in an important job interview, sitting with her legs crossed and her hands folded neatly on her knee. Yes, she looks professional, even respectful, but there's a hidden message coming through: She's on her best behavior. She's carefully monitoring her image. All of her body language signals are in check. Sadly, the more intent she is on making a good impression, the less impression she's making. Not until she relaxes and gets her hands more involved in the conversation does the interviewer gets a better picture of who she is.

GESTURE CODE #2
Engage your gestures from the beginning of the conversation

When we feel perfectly comfortable, when we let down our guard, our hands naturally engage. If you want to give the *impression* you are perfectly comfortable or want to help your listeners let down *their* guard, get your own hands moving. What we do with our body language tends to indicate the relationship we have with the person across from us. Interactive hand gestures imply that the relationship has already been established. Hands folded politely may indicate some reservation to participate or, referring back to the poker metaphor, to show your hand.

Here's the bottom line: If you want to appear comfortable and unguarded, your gestures need to start talking when your mouth begins moving. A key "tell" of self-consciousness is when the mouth is moving but no other body language signal is yet engaged.

> *If you want to appear comfortable and unguarded, your gestures need to start talking when your mouth begins moving.*

GESTURE CODE #3
Reach out to your listener

So we're back to the question, "What do I do with my hands?" You should reach out. Literally. A brief examination of social behavior reveals that human beings primarily use three types of hand gestures: the reach, the show, and the chop.

The reach: The first and most natural looking gesture is the "reach." It's a simple movement in which you subtly extend your hand toward the person you're talking to, almost as if you are gently handing your listener a piece of information. If you observe people talking for any length of time, you'll see it happen again and again. We literally reach out to each other when speaking. Keep in mind that the reach doesn't mean you push your arm into someone's personal space; it's just a simple gesture in the listener's direction.

The show: The second gesture is the "show." For example, when describing something very tall, you might raise your hand to indicate the height. When talking about a fender bender, you might smack your hands together for effect. While saying that the room is too hot and stuffy, you might unconsciously fan your face. Our hands are often visual aids in the conversation, helping illustrate the point.

The chop: Finally, there's the "chop." For emphasis, your hand chops downward through the air to punctuate your words. It helps you emphasize how strongly you feel about your point. Our politicians frequently do this on the campaign trail, as I'm sure you've noticed.

While all three are good tools to have at your disposal, the safest and most natural is the reach. The show has to be used sparingly or you risk looking like a schoolteacher talking to toddlers or, worse yet, a mime. And a light touch is needed with the chop or you may come across as too emphatic, pushy, or aggressive. The chop is kind of like typing in all caps. When it's done every now and then to emphasize your point, it can be helpful. Done as a matter of habit, it becomes annoying.

GESTURE CODE #4
Keep your hands in the gesture box

Now that you know what types of hand gestures work best, let's define the actual airspace your hands should occupy. Effective gesturing takes place inside the "gesture box." Your hands should typically gesture no higher than your sternum, no lower than your hip joints, and no wider than the width of your shoulders. The sweet spot or the bull's-eye is your navel. Gestures that initiate from the navel tend to look the most natural. Use the space in front of you from your navel forward about 12 inches.

To look comfortable, be sure that your arms and hands are moving loosely. Avoid what I call the T-rex: Don't pin your elbows to your sides and gesture with only your forearms. Allow a bit of air under your elbows.

As we speak, our hands typically engage and rest intermittently. If your hands are taking a break, you can fold them loosely in the general vacinity of your navel. It's rare that a full sentence will go by without some sort of gesturing to support your thought. If two or three sentences go by without gesturing, the speaker is almost certainly in masking mode.

When gestures are distracting, it's usually for one of two reasons: The gestures are too repetitive or are consistently outside of the gesture box. Only an honest self-evaluation using a video camera will show if you have one of these habits, and I'll go into detail about how to do that in chapter 8 (Self-evaluation). However, if you find that you're overly fond of a particular gesture, it's time to create new patterns. Check out the highlight box below for suggestions. The most common repetitive gesture is the chop, so be especially cautious or, as noted above, you risk coming across as too emphatic or aggressive.

To avoid the mistake of gesturing consistently outside of the box, the key word here is *consistently*. It's fine, even encouraged, to reach outside of the box occasionally to show passion and enthusiasm. Gestures consistently outside the box, however, will soon become distracting for listeners.

Note that the size of the gesture box changes from culture to culture, generally in proportion to the amount of emotion appropriately displayed in public. In Japan, for example, people have a fairly small gesture box, while Italians use a fairly large gesture box. In all cultures, though, the sweet spot is still the navel area. If you initiate your gestures from that spot, you are likely to look comfortable no matter how big the gesture box.

Practice exercise: Break the repetition

If you're stuck in a repetitive pattern of gesturing, try adding some variety to your style. Spend a few minutes rehearsing your sales message, reciting poetry, or giving your opinion of the world news while focusing on your gestures. It helps if you practice this while standing in front of a full-length mirror.

If you tend to gesture in an up-and-down pattern, practice moving your hands from side to side. If you tend to use very large gestures, keep your hands in a smaller box. If you tend to be very symmetrical, try using one hand at a time. And most importantly, if your gestures tend to be outward-bound chops, turn them around to pull people toward you rather than push them away. Once you feel comfortable using your hands in a variety of ways, step away from the mirror and practice for a few moments without the visual input.

The exception to the rule

Once you know the ground rules for hand gesturing, feel free to break them when it's more appropriate. Gesturing always looks more comfortable than a masking position; but in some instances, you will be more effective if your hands are still. For example, you wouldn't do lots of gesturing in very formal situations or where protocol is traditional, such as when you're offering a funeral eulogy or giving a State of the Union address. Or, if you were meeting a foreign dignitary, you would show your respect by keeping your hands relaxed by your sides or loosely folded in front of you.

Another instance is when you need to portray yourself as resolute and unchanging. I remember watching a press conference with four women who were suing their employer for gender discrimination. All four sat perfectly still with their hands folded neatly on their laps. This was an excellent strategy for showing they weren't flexible and weren't going to budge on the issue.

Here's my point: Interactive gesturing helps build relationships. If your primary goal is to look formal, polite, or immovable, you might do well to keep you hands still. If you'd like to look interactive, fluid, and connected, get your hands moving.

Making it second nature

There's still a lingering concern with changing your gesturing habits: Intentionally talking with your hands can feel so unnatural.

I'm not suggesting that you focus on your hands while speaking. In a perfect world, your body language would be fully engaged without any conscious thought. But we should have a strategy in place for those moments when we aren't acting perfectly natural, especially if we might slip into masking mode. Your goal is to nudge your hands into action so they will quickly take on a life of their own.

The only way to remedy this situation is to practice. Intentionally get your hands engaged . . . even when it's not important. The more you do it *intentionally*, the less conversation your brain will have about it when it matters. You'll be learning how to engage your natural body language without derailing your thought process.

Take a field trip to a social gathering

Venture outside of your office and challenge yourself. Find a place with lots of social action, such as a cocktail party, a networking meeting, or the coffee hour following your religious service. With the mindset of a social anthropologist, take a few moments to observe what people are doing with their hands. You'll notice when people become engaged in lively, dynamic conversations because their hands are lively and dynamic as well. The more comfortable two people seem to be with each other, the more interactive their gestures will be.

Next, step into the mix yourself. Have a conversation with someone nearby while trying to get your hands engaged. You may feel somewhat awkward when gesturing intentionally but keep it up. As you chat, continue to focus on keeping your hands engaged; within 15 minutes or so, the self-conscious feeling will melt away. Practice this in low-risk environments as often as possible. When the stakes are higher, all you will need is a quick mental reminder to kick-start your natural gestures.

Face value

Just as our hands participate interactively when we feel comfortable in conversations, our facial muscles do the same. We move fluidly from one natural facial gesture to the next, and this animation plays a significant role in conveying meaning and intention.

As listeners, we don't just listen to the speaker's words; we read his or her face, too. Doing so helps us understand the context of what is being said: Is she serious or joking? Is he being emotional or factual? Is this important or trivial? Our expressions verify our words.

Facial fluidity is also a key signal of trustworthiness. In his book *Emotions Revealed*, Paul Ekman, a world-renowned expert in facial expressions, tells us that our faces move easily from one gesture to another in natural conversation. True emotion and expressions happen fairly quickly, so any expressions held for too long may look manipulative, protective, or, to use my terminology, masked.

> *As listeners, we don't just listen to the speaker's words; we read his or her face, too. Doing so helps us understand the context of what is being said: Is she serious or joking? Is he being emotional or factual?*

When we're uncomfortable or self-conscious, we often slip into *facial masking*. We restrict the natural movement of our facial gestures, holding our expression in one position. People tend to lock into various masks depending on what they're comfortable with.

One end of the spectrum is the smiling mask. The initial impression can be friendly, but the locked-on nature of the smile soon reveals discomfort. The other end of the spectrum is the poker face. Showing no expression leaves it up to the listener to decipher the context behind the words. Both ends of the spectrum are protective.

Excessive smiling is a product of what psychologists call the "tend-and-befriend" response. Under pressure, this automatic-pilot response drives us to make friends with an enemy, sending a message that says, "I'm no threat to you." (For more information, read the section about "self-commenting," page 93 in chapter 5.) Some individuals become so habitual about smiling that they can't hold a conversation without doing it, no matter the context. While this response may help us appear more inviting or approachable, it can seriously undermine our appearance of authority and confidence. The solution, of course, is to learn to relax the facial muscles.

The poker-face mask is also a defense mechanism. Just as people will restrict and conceal their body language signals under pressure, the face can tighten up, too. The solution is learning to show more "friendship signals." These are gestures that create interaction with the listener —nodding, raising the eyebrows, opening the eyes wider, changing expressions, reaching toward the listener, and, especially, smiling. The smile is a universal signal of friendliness. While it's true smiling can be taken too far, it is an important skill for those who rely too much on the poker face.

I'm not suggesting that you be manipulative about your facial gestures. Relying on your natural impulses will produce a much more genuine result. However, it's important to note that facial masking is a common, automatic-pilot response to stress. The next time you have a little adrenaline flowing, take a moment to notice your face, pay attention to any tension you may have, and consciously try to stay fluid.

Case studies: Jack and Annie face facts

When Jack walked into my workshop, I was immediately struck by his presence. He had a deep baritone voice and one of the most rigid poker faces I'd ever encountered. Jack sold heavy equipment—forklifts, tractors, and backhoes. He was at ease in the field talking with farmers and construction workers but found communicating with his co-workers in the sales office less rewarding and more difficult.

As is the routine in my workshops, I invited him to walk to the front of the room and introduce himself while I videotaped. His words were cordial, but his face was like stone. I asked him a few questions to see if I could loosen him up. Even when he described a funny story about his toddler, his face stayed remarkably still, no hint of a smile, no lift of an eyebrow, no change of expression whatsoever.

When I asked him about his objectives, he confessed that he had a hard time connecting with people socially. He didn't know why. He thought he was a nice enough guy. When I showed him his videotape, he was floored. He had no idea that his outward appearance was so stern. He confessed he was actually *trying* to be expressive because he was being videotaped.

The solution was obvious: He needed to show some friendship signals. Back at the front of the room, I instructed Jack to introduce himself again, this time deliberately trying to smile. He tried, but I saw no discernible difference. I asked him to try again and to be even more obvious. He did, but I still saw very little difference. This time, I asked him to exaggerate wildly, to force himself to be over-the-top, unrealistically friendly. He did, and the corners of his mouth curled up into a very slight smile. For the first time in the workshop, he looked mildly friendly. The class applauded and threw accolades in his direction. However, he shook his head and said, "I feel like a clown."

His facial expressions had frozen to such a state that even the slightest movements felt extreme and inappropriate. This is an example of how one's internal perception can sometimes be severely out of sync with the external impression.

I sent Jack home with a regimen of facial exercises to get his muscles activated again. I advised him to get a video camera and to practice with it for five minutes a day so he could benefit from a more accurate view of himself. Since he had a young child at home, I suggested that when reading to her, he act out the stories and make the characters bigger than life. Finally, I encouraged him to develop the new habit of expressiveness by practicing in low-risk interactions, as when ordering his deli sandwich or chatting with the checkout clerk. Jack and I stayed in touch and met sometime later. Jack's outward image was soon much more in sync with how he wished to be perceived.

Jack was an interesting and challenging case, but he changed. Likewise, Annie's story is interesting, but it is at the other end of the facial masking spectrum. On first meeting Annie, the adjectives that sprang to mind were *nice, friendly, bubbly,* and *accommodating*. If she were a tour guide or a receptionist, these attributes would have matched her job perfectly.

But Annie was an attorney with aspirations of being a trial lawyer. Her brilliant grasp of the law had served her well in law school, placing her top of her class. But in the reality of her fast-paced, hard-edged, sink-or-swim law firm, she could not convince her colleagues of her abilities. She felt doomed to a life of writing legal briefs in back offices.

Annie's problem? She couldn't stop smiling. She was a victim of the "tend-and-befriend" response. While her smiling was especially pronounced in stressful conversations, it had become a habit following her everywhere she went. Because her chosen profession was fraught with high-pressure situations, it was time to handle the issue.

The solution was to desensitize Annie by deliberately identifying situations that cued her smiling response. Since this behavior tends to increase when an individual feels singled out, I made sure she was the first person on camera in my workshop that day. At first, just introducing herself without smiling was a problem, but soon her face relaxed. Next, I pushed the issue by having her address topics she might find difficult to discuss. I asked her to describe a time when she did something embarrassing, when she broke the rules, and when she hurt someone's feelings. I instructed her to make up something outrageous about herself but to describe it as if it were true. I invited her to brag about herself, to say something critical about someone else, or to reveal a secret dream. Once she could handle all of these conversations without reverting to the smiling behavior, she was ready to take it out into the real world.

It's important to note that you can have a pleasant expression on your face without actually smiling. I encouraged Annie to practice this in her office by giving some lightweight feedback to a colleague, striking up a casual conversation with a senior partner, or asking her supervisor for the afternoon off. We connected after she had practiced for several weeks. I found the new Annie to be the pleasant yet assertive woman she knew herself to be.

Practice exercise: Put your best face forward

If you think you might have a problem with a lack of facial expressions, here's how to practice on your own. Spend an entire weekend greeting everyone you meet with a smile. Start with your family and friends. They'll love your positive attitude. Then get out of the house so you can interact with neighbors, waiters, and shoppers. Smile at dogs and children. Finally, intentionally strike up a cheerful conversation with the person in line next to you at the coffee shop and consciously keep your face engaged.

Practice on the phone by taking a tip from professional telemarketers. Their desks are often equipped with mirrors to reflect their face and hand gestures. Not only is it a gentle reminder to stay actively engaged, but the "friendship signals" they display in their body language have a tendency to come through in their voices.

Take a field trip to the mall

If you are concerned with excessive smiling, take a field trip to the mall. Interact with as many clerks, waiters, and shoppers as possible while keeping your face relaxed. Ask another shopper for directions or a restaurant recommendation. Ask the sales clerk for more details about the products she's selling. See if you can be very pleasant without actually smiling at the individual. Finally, put your skills to the test by taking on more difficult conversations. Give your waiter a special instruction for your meal or return something you've purchased without offering an explanation, all the while keeping your face relaxed.

Moving on

Now that you have a clearer idea of how your body language can help you send a message of crediblity and confidence, focus on your vocal track. It's not accidental that we describe someone who has great influence as having a "powerful voice." What does your voice say about your ability to get the job done? How can you make sure that your voice is serving you well?

*To watch a short video of the author
demonstrating the skills in this chapter,
scan the box above or
enter this URL into your browser.*

www.thecredibilitycode.com/video/gztv62

CHAPTER 3

Vocal Skills:
Finding Your Voice

"Words mean more than what is set down on paper.
It takes the human voice to infuse them
with deeper meaning."

– MAYA ANGELOU

In one memorable episode of *Seinfeld,* Jerry and Elaine are dining out with Kramer and his latest girlfriend. She's a fashion designer who has a habit of talking in an extremely low volume. Her volume is so low that no one except Kramer, who is sitting right next to her, can understand a word she says.

Jerry and Elaine do their best. They continually ask her to repeat herself, but eventually they give up, not wanting to appear rude. They resort to smiling politely, nodding, and saying, "Uh-huh."

At one point, Kramer leaves the table. In his desperation to converse politely with the woman, Jerry unwittingly agrees to something the "low talker" asks. Only later does he realize that he has promised to wear a ludicrous, puffy white shirt designed by Kramer's girlfriend for his upcoming appearance on the *Today* show.

Jerry Seinfeld's genius is taking the moments of frustration we all experience in everyday life and expanding them into full-blown comic routines. We've all experienced a low talker. And after asking the person to speak up once or twice, we revert to nodding politely, hoping that we are responding appropriately to what they are saying. In extreme cases, we may actively avoid this individual to escape the discomfort of the situation.

We all want our "voice to be heard." It's not an accident that we describe someone who has great influence in the community as having a "powerful voice." The idioms we use in our language clearly articulate the codes of conduct for appearing credible and confident. To have influence, you must learn to "speak up for yourself." To be described as articulate and well spoken, you must literally articulate clearly and speak well.

Vocal Codes of Conduct

- Speak with optimal volume.
- Articulate clearly.
- Keep your pacing relaxed.
- Highlight your message with expression.
- Engage your diaphragm for resonance.

Adequate versus optimal

To be understood, you must meet some basic needs for your listener: Your volume must be adequate, your articulation must be clear, and your pace must be appropriate. However, there's a big difference between being technically audible and truly making a connection. And this is the area where most people have the greatest opportunity for growth. To convey confidence, you need to understand the distinction between adequate and optimal.

Most people have a vocal range of effectiveness that falls between below average and truly exceptional. When I'm evaluating participants in my workshops, I rate each of their skills on a scale from one to five:

1—Absent, 2—Below average, 3—Adequate, 4—Optimal, 5—Too much. Here are the descriptions for volume levels:

1. **Absent**—The speaker is inaudible.
2. **Below average**—We can barely hear the speaker even when we concentrate.
3. **Adequate**—We can technically hear the speaker as long as we pay attention.
4. **Optimal**—We can hear every word the speaker says without any effort.
5. **Too much**—The speaker is overpowering.

As it turns out, most people's vocal skills are a level 3 on this scale: Adequate. That's both good news and bad news. It means you can understand them, but they aren't exactly enticing you to listen. Ask yourself this question: Is "adequate" acceptable? Is it an adjective you want people to use in describing you?

What holds most people back is the fear of becoming a level 5: Overpowering. When people come on too strong, the listener shuts down or puts up boundaries. Level 5 is not an effective style for building relationships, and most of us have experienced discomfort or embarrassment for someone who comes on too strong. We may have consciously or semiconsciously made an agreement with ourselves never to make that mistake. As a consequence, people navigate themselves into the average zone to be polite or to not offend. Level 3 is the risk-free zone.

If you want to rise above the crowd, however, you'll want to make sure that all of your skills are in the optimal range. Unless you consistently receive feedback that you are too loud, too bold, or too much, you can safely assume that you can take your skills up a notch.

VOCAL CODE #1
Speak with optimal volume

The most common problems with one's volume are speaking too softly or dropping volume at the ends of phrases or sentences. How loudly you speak is often an indicator of how comfortable you feel. As mentioned in chapter 1, we take up more physical space when we feel comfortable and less space when we feel uncomfortable.

The same is true for volume. The more comfortable you feel, the louder you tend to be. Those who speak in a strong, clear voice tend to sound the most at ease and self-assured. And ironically, people whose friends or family tell them they are overly loud at parties will often over-compensate by speaking too softly in business settings.

Of all the skills I address in this chapter, the easiest skill to adjust is volume. And because volume has such a big impact on how confident you appear, it offers the easiest return on building skills. By just optimizing this one behavior, you may take yourself from good to great.

When it comes to how listeners assess voices, in general, the stronger the volume, the more confident and authoritative the person comes across. The softer the volume, the softer or weaker the person seems.

It's not a mystery: It takes a strong body to produce a strong voice, which is one reason people with strong voices are perceived as more powerful. It takes muscle—specifically the diaphragm muscle—and a certain amount of self-assuredness to speak up; a stronger volume sends a message of confidence.

If you know your voice is weak or you consistently receive feedback that your voice is small or quiet, your plan of action should be clear: Develop your voice. This chapter includes exercises to help you build a stronger voice, but, in a perfect world, you'd work with a vocal coach. Please don't think of taking voice lessons or doing exercises as a punishment for being deficient; think of it as an opportunity to differentiate yourself from the crowd. Nearly every celebrity, newscaster, politician, or CEO in the public eye has worked with a speaking coach. It's not a punishment; it's an advantage.

Ability versus willingness

When I'm coaching people to increase their volume, two primary issues come up. The first is their *ability* to speak with a stronger volume, and the second is their *willingness* to speak with a stronger volume.

As far as ability is concerned, most people are physically capable of speaking louder when asked to. People often speak too softly because they simply aren't aware that louder would be better.

More often than not, it's laziness—not a lazy individual but a lazy diaphragm. As a matter of economy, our bodies will take the path of least resistance. Without a clear understanding of the benefit of being louder, our bodies will put in the least amount of effort required to complete the task at hand. Thus, we lean toward being adequate instead of optimal. The solution is to gain more strength and stamina in the diaphragm. If the core muscle is stronger, you will naturally speak with a stronger voice without feeling as if it takes extra effort.

Addressing one's *willingness* to speak louder is a little more difficult. People who consistently speak in an inappropriately low volume have a meter problem: Their internal meter of how loud they are speaking is out of sync with their external meter. They think they are speaking much more loudly than they are. Even if these speakers can produce more volume, they are reluctant to do so because they don't want to speak inappropriately loud. When I ask them to increase their volume to what sounds like average volume to the rest of us, they are convinced they are shouting. Since no one wants to be obnoxiously loud, the low talker will increase volume only marginally when asked to speak up.

In this instance, a small-group workshop is more powerful than one-on-one coaching. When I alone mention someone's volume is too soft, it's just my observations against that person's experience. When eight other workshop participants are nodding their heads "yes" and claiming the volume is too soft, the speaker begins to acknowledge the difference between his or her personal perception and the perception of others.

Flex your diaphragm muscle

Speaking with a strong confident voice starts with proper breath support. The more energy you put into your breath, the more energized you'll sound. Yet most people have never been taught proper breath support, and that means most people have a lazy diaphragm.

> *The good news is that you aren't stuck with a weak voice. Anyone can have a powerful voice; you just have to be willing to do the heavy lifting to get it.*

The diaphragm is the engine responsible for volume and breath support. It's a muscle about the size of your fist that sits at the bottom of your ribcage underneath the lungs. Have you been working your diaphragm lately? Not likely. But the diaphragm is a muscle that can be exercised and developed just like any other muscle. To do so, you need to put it under some stress with five minutes of isolated exercises each day. What are those five minutes a day worth to you?

When volume is too loud

Based on experience in my workshops, I've discovered some interesting patterns. One in 5 people typically speaks too softly, while 1 in 200 people speaks too loudly. Soft talkers are significantly more common than loud talkers, yet most people are afraid of coming on too strong. This makes sense because in most cultures, it's more socially acceptable to speak softly than loudly, and loud people can leave an indelible impression.

One evening, my husband and I were having dinner at an upscale bistro. Three people came in and were seated five booths away from us. We were the only two groups in the restaurant. One of the men in the party began to speak so loudly we could hear everything he said as if he were sitting at the table with us. At one point, he began telling the story of how he accidentally cut off his thumb with a chain saw. Our dinners arrived just as he started going into detail about the amount of blood and how he called 911.

Practice exercise: Strengthen your diaphragm

To engage your diaphragm, say "shush" forcefully, as if you were trying to get the attention of someone in the next room. Stretch the word out for about three seconds—"shushhhhhhh." Can you feel how the muscle under your ribcage contracts each time? That's your diaphragm, and to strengthen it, try the following exercises.

- Say the days of the week all in one breath, drawing out the vowels so the diaphragm can't rest in between words. Once you've done that a couple of times, try saying the months of the year in one breath.

- Make a list of things you plan to buy at the store and recite the list aloud without pausing for air. Repeat this exercise several times, adding an item to the list each time. Be sure to emphasize the final word in each phrase to keep your diaphragm engaged all the way to the end. Here's an example:

  "I went to the store and bought some eggs."
  "I went to the store and bought some eggs and milk."
  "I went to the store and bought some eggs, milk, and cheese."

- Count from one to five all in one breath, getting incrementally louder with each word. Say "one" as if you're speaking to someone just 2 feet away, then gradually increase the volume so you're saying the number "five" as if to someone 30 feet away. Don't allow your pitch to get higher with each number and be sure to keep your larynx relaxed. All of the effort to increase your volume should come from your diaphragm muscle.

- Read out loud for three to four minutes, focusing on keeping your diaphragm contracted the entire time. Breathe whenever you need to, but otherwise keep a slight but steady pressure on your diaphragm, as if you were playing a bagpipe or an accordion.

As you might expect, he made it difficult for us to enjoy our meal. This man clearly had no idea he was speaking too loudly; he was blind to his own behavior. Unfortunately I'm sure his behavior was not restricted just to this one evening; he likely speaks too loudly habitually.

My advice is the same whether you speak too softly or too loudly: Pay attention to the feedback you get from others. If people consistently say that you are too soft or too loud or that you mumble or speak too quickly, they are probably right, and you should work to break the habit. Unsolicited feedback is very difficult to give, so if people are taking the risk to tell you about your undesirable behavior, it must be having an impact on your communication . . . and your credibility.

VOCAL CODE #2
Articulate clearly

In the movie *The Great Debaters*, Denzel Washington's character is the debate coach for an all-black university, and he is preparing his team for a championship competition that will pit his students against the all-white Harvard team. During an intense training session, the students stand on the edge of a pond with corks in their mouths reciting tongue twisters and poems while the coach sits in a boat that drifts farther and farther away. The challenge forces the students not only to project their voices but also to precisely articulate their words in spite of physical obstacles. As a result, they articulate impressively in their culminating debate.

Articulation is the process of using the lips, tongue, teeth, and jaw to produce *the sounds of speech*—the consonants and vowels. In general, the more crisply you enunciate your words, the more intelligent and the more attentive to detail you'll sound. The more lazily you articulate your words, the less intelligent and less credible others will perceive you.

When we describe someone as articulate, we generally mean they express their thoughts well. But it is amazing how the technical skill of clearly enunciating will help you come across as more articulate in the metaphoric sense. The good news is you can take control over the technical skill of articulation. With just a few minutes of practice each day, you can transform your articulation from adequate to optimal.

Improving your articulation is all about muscle memory—getting your speaking muscles to work habitually in a more rigorous way. A quick fix is simply to open your mouth wider. Have you heard the expression "tight-lipped" and "close-mouthed"? These expressions are often used to mean "reserved" or "reticent." To come across as more *open* to listeners, *open* your mouth wider when you speak. This one change can move your articulation from average to good. To elevate to "excellent," put your muscles through a regular workout.

It's been my experience that only 1 in 50 people speaks with optimal articulation. So unless you regularly get compliments on the clarity of your speech, it is likely you have merely adequate articulation. However, if people regularly ask you to speak more clearly or to repeat yourself, it is likely that your articulation is below average. Almost everyone reading this book would benefit from sharper articulation.

Case Study: Anthony sharpens his image

My first interaction with Anthony was over the phone when he called to inquire about one of my workshops. When he told me he was a wealth manager, in charge of millions of dollars of other people's money, I thought he was joking. His mode of articulation was so mumbled and immature that I thought I was speaking to a teenage boy. Even when he listed some of his awards and successes, I had a hard time believing he was a professional. His auditory image was so out of sync with his credentials that everything he said about himself sounded like bravado. Anthony was sure that his youth was holding him back from reaching his full potential. I was convinced it was his articulation.

When we finally met at a workshop, Anthony's visual image was quite different. Yes, he was young, but he was also tall, athletic, and exceedingly well dressed. His bright, expressive demeanor made him a star in the room, and I realized he had not padded his resume.

Nonetheless, I suspected prospective clients whose initial interactions with him were over the phone were not likely to give him a chance until they met him in person. Anthony needed to improve his articulation so his true expertise had a chance to shine through.

I started by having Anthony warm up the muscles of his face. Runners, gymnasts, and volleyball players all warm up key muscle groups before they practice; the same is true for articulation. Then I asked him to cover some typical investment advice while opening his mouth wider than usual. He complied, and just this one change made a significant difference in his clarity. Anthony was sure that this behavior must look ridiculous to others, but because of the workshop setting, I was able to allay his fears. The other participants' unanimous feedback indicated that he not only sounded more articulate, but he also looked more professional.

While opening the mouth is important, *closing* the mouth around the words is just as vital. To help with this, I brought out the stir sticks. Gripping a stick between his front teeth, I asked Anthony to continue with his message, wrapping his lips around every consonant. The stir stick creates a significant impediment, and the muscles have to work 10 times harder to produce the sounds. Even so, every time he slurred a word, I made him stop and repeat that word clearly. At first, I stopped him every four or five words. But soon, he was completing full sentences without an error. Then came one of my favorite moments in any workshop: I had him remove the stick but continue to speak as if the stick were still there. The class was floored: His articulation was impeccable! In the course of 10 minutes, he had taken this skill from poor to exceptional.

I sent him home with the instruction to do these very same drills five minutes a day for the next month. When I spoke with him on the phone a couple of months later, his transformation was complete. He sounded like the expert adviser he truly was.

Practice exercise: Warm up your facial muscles

Spend about 60 seconds warming up your articulator muscles, which are the muscles directly responsible for speech. It's the same principle you would use in warming up clay before starting to sculpt with it.

- Alternate between pursing your lips and sneering.
- Scrunch all of your facial features into your nose.
- Try to spread all of your facial features to the edge of your face.
- Blow air through your lips (as if imitating a horse).
- Open your mouth as wide as possible.
- Stretch your tongue back and forward in various positions.
- Move your tongue over and around all your teeth.
- Massage your jaw muscles with your fingers.
- Pretend to chew something big and gristly.

Practice exercise: Challenge your articulators

Say the following articulation drills several times. Make sure to open your mouth wider than usual and hit every consonant as cleanly as possible. Keep your attention on how the words feel in your mouth. Start by over-articulating each word and then try to say the same phrase as quickly as possible while keeping the clarity. If you start to slur the sounds or trip up, slow down . . . and try again.

- Clickity, clickity, clickity, clack
- Ricky, ticky, ticky tick
- Niminy, piminy, niminy piminy
- Topeka, Bodega, Topeka, Bodega
- Peggy Babcock, Peggy Babcock
- Will you, William, wait? Will you wait?
- Red leather, yellow leather, good blood, bad blood
- She stood on the balcony hiccupping, amicably welcoming him.
- Whether the weather is cold, or whether the weather is hot,
  we'll be together whatever the weather, whether we like it or not.

Practice exercise: Grip a stir stick

An excellent way to retrain your articulator muscles is to make them work overtime. Take a stir stick or a pencil, grip it between your front teeth, and run through the articulation drills again. Work so hard to speak clearly that a person in the next room wouldn't be able to tell that you have a stir stick between your teeth. Then spend a minute reading something out loud—poetry, prose, the newspaper—making sure every word is understandable. Last, remove the stick and continue reading, using the same effort to produce the sounds.

VOCAL CODE #3

Keep your pacing relaxed

When watching scary movies in my younger years, I would often fast-forward though the suspenseful parts. Instead of watching the heroine tiptoe down the creaky hallway and slowly open the rusty attic door, she'd waddle comically back and forth, fling the door open, and melodramatically throw her hands up in surprise when a dead body tumbled out. The pace, or tempo, of any interaction can have a big impact on its mood and credibility.

Your speaking pace, or words per minute, affects the tone and credibility of your content. It's similar to how the tempo of music affects the mood of the performance. Any piece of music has a range of tempo that is appropriate for the separate movements, and the same is true for spoken language. Generally, the faster the pace, the more upbeat and positive the message; the slower the pace, the more calm, serene, or serious it is. Speak too fast, and it becomes frenetic or comic; speak too slowly, and it becomes tedious or boring. A comfortable listening pace is about 170 words per minute, give or take 10 words or so in either direction, depending on the mood.

Remember that the pace of your speech will affect how the listener perceives you. The more slowly you speak, the more confident and authoritative you come across; your message is important, and you have the authority to take up the listener's time. Conversely, the more quickly you speak, the less confident you seem. A fast pace is often associated with an infusion of adrenalin, so a person who speaks quickly can appear to be nervous.

> *The more quickly you speak, the less confident you seem. A fast pace is often associated with an infusion of adrenalin, so a person who speaks quickly can appear to be nervous.*

The most common pacing problem is people who talk too quickly. It's a rare individual who speaks too slowly, and even then the problem is usually a lack of energy or too many filler words *(ahh, ya' know, like, ummm)*.

A fast speaking pace is a common problem in business settings. Time runs over, and you have less time to present your ideas than planned. In this situation, most people will speed up and try to say everything faster. Sadly, this lowers listener retention, and you are likely to look more nervous and less prepared. Imagine you are at a concert that is running long: Would it be effective for the conductor to play the last three songs 50 percent faster? It is best to cut some content than to deliver poorly the information you have.

Slowing down will do many positive things for your image. You will appear more in control, and your audience will have more time to digest the message. Nonetheless, we tend to speed up when we feel less secure with our content. But this is the very time when it would be helpful to slow down to collect and order our thoughts more effectively. Slowing down also makes it easier to eliminate those useless filler sounds.

The power of the pause

It's the novice graphic designer who fills every corner of the page with information. The experienced graphic designer understands that white space helps sell the message. Be willing to add a little temporal white space to your conversation. Do not fear the pause. As Mark Twain once said, "The right word may be effective, but no word was ever as effective as a rightly timed pause."

We think that if we pause we will appear less intelligent or prepared, or even as boring. Research confirms the exact opposite: People who pause more in their conversations come across as more intelligent and better prepared.

From the speaker's point of view, a pause can seem unbearably long. From the listeners' point of view, pauses are quite comfortable. It's good customer service for listeners because they have the chance to lock the information away. And remember to let a well-placed pause be a pause; don't ruin it with darting eyes or filler noise. Allow a moment of silence to work its retentive power.

> *People who pause more in their conversations come across as more intelligent and better prepared.*

Pausing also shows you have command of the conversation. Many people fear that if they pause they will be interrupted. And, yes, listeners might well jump in at a pause if the sound of your words is the only clue that you are still speaking. But if all the other positive attributes of your speaking style are present—direct eye contact, strong posture, speaking with expression—listeners will see you're not finished and wait for you to continue.

As a side note, depending on the geographical region and demographic, the speaking pace of the general population may vary. In the United States, urban New Yorkers tends to be on the fast side, while rural Georgians tend to speak more slowly. People in their twenties enjoy a faster listening pace than people in their fifties. Of course, these are generalizations: Individuals vary. But it's important to consider these differences when communicating. If you speak at about 170 words per minute, your pace will be appropriate just about anywhere you go.

Practice exercise: Test your words per minute

Test your own speaking rate by reading the following paragraph at a pace you think is energized but not rushed. Since a comfortable listening pace is about 170 words per minute, it should take you about 60 seconds to read aloud. If your pace is more than a few seconds fast or slow, practice reading the paragraph until you can more closely achieve a 60-second pace.

Reading test—171 words

A manufacturer of flooring materials needed to increase market share. Management was about to launch an incentive program to boost dealer sales. But during a planning session, the operations manager wisely observed that his department would need to increase its skilled labor force and upgrade equipment to handle increased sales volumes. He remembered flat sales years that prompted a downsizing in operations. The incentive meeting came to a cold, stark halt.

One manager bolted to the white board. Other department managers jumped in to add their own details to a rough flow chart of the company's overall business cycle, from the purchase of raw materials to after-sale customer service. The revised flow chart revealed that a plan to increase sales, implemented without considering all aspects of their business cycle flow, *would disrupt several areas of the business.*

The firm's management began improving all points in their business cycle until they were certain they could process additional sales. Only then did they begin what became a successful incentive program for their dealers.

Dawson, Robert S. (2009) *The Secret to Incentive Program Success: Incentive ROI That Makes Bean Counters Smile!* TBG Publications.

Practice exercise: Insert a two-snap pause

One way to practice pausing is to add a two-second pause at the end of each thought. Take a moment to describe your hometown or read a passage aloud from a book, snapping your fingers twice at the end of each sentence. The idea is to get comfortable coming to a complete stop.

When I lead this exercise in my workshops, I do the snapping while the participant speaks. While this pause can seem inordinately long to some speakers, especially if they're used to rushing, inevitably the workshop participants report it's far easier to absorb the message with the pauses inserted.

VOCAL CODE #4
Highlight your message with expression

Vocal expression brings your conversation to life. Using tools such as pitch, pace, inflection, emphasis, and emotional range, you "translate" your message for listeners. Like using a highlighter pen to identify what's noteworthy in a written passage, vocal expression helps listeners better understand what's important. The more expression in your voice, the more personable and engaging you come across.

Watching a bad actor deliver a Shakespearean soliloquy can be painfully boring. Even though he may be speaking English (granted, old English), it's as if he's speaking an entirely different language. A brilliant actor can deliver the same lines, and we understand the meaning as well as the emotion and subtext. We are transported from just trying to understand to truly enjoying the communication. Great actors are masters at vocal expression.

Vocal expression is also crucial to meaning. A capable speaker uses verbal punctuation the way writers add commas and periods. Listeners rely on this verbal punctuation to tell them where ideas begin and end, and which information is most important.

The quick fix for bringing out more expression in the voice is to turn up your overall level of energy. Increase your volume. Punch the key words more sharply. Intentionally show more animation in your face and hands. Stretch for a wider range of inflection. In short, throw the message a little harder to the listener.

While it's easy to say some people are more expressive than others, expression is a habit like any other skill. The more you deliberately ask yourself to be expressive, the more naturally it will come to you when it matters.

Practice exercise: Add a little stress

Read the sentences below aloud, giving each highlighted word a little extra emphasis. Note how the stress brings new meaning to the sentence each time.

She placed the book on my desk.
She **placed** the book on my desk.
She placed the **book** on my desk.
She placed the book **on** my desk.
She placed the book on **my** desk.
She placed the book on my **desk**.

Now, use a highlighting pen to shade the key words of a piece of writing near you, such as a newspaper, an email, or your upcoming presentation, and read it aloud. Notice how the added emphasis makes the message more dynamic.

Practice exercise: Play Mad Gab

The board game *Mad Gab* lists combinations of words that look like nonsense, but when pronounced aloud, sound like familiar phrases. The sounds are all present, but the punctuation has been deliberately removed, making the game fun (and difficult). The game points out just how important stress, inflection, and pause can be.

For example, how do you say the phrase "Law-sand-jealous"? When you say it out loud, the actual phrase is "Los Angeles." Here are more examples:

- "Wheel yum air ream he." Say it out loud, and it becomes "Will you marry me?"

- "Palm hick heart knee." Say it out loud, and it becomes "Paul McCartney."

- "Age oar chip each." Say it out loud, and it becomes "a Georgia peach."

Play this game to gain a deeper understanding of the importance of vocal variety.

VOCAL CODE #5
Engage your diaphragm for resonance

In the 1952 comedy *Singin' in the Rain*, the beautiful yet ditzy leading lady of silent films is trying to make the transition into talking pictures. But she has a problem. Her speaking voice grates like fingernails on a chalkboard: screechy, shrill, and nasally. Desperate to keep her star status, she blackmails the studio executives into putting her into a talkie by dubbing her voice with the dulcet tones of another actress. Eventually, when the deception is revealed, the silent star flees in disgrace, and her stand-in becomes the star—and gets the handsome leading man.

This may be just a film storyline, but having poor vocal quality can affect you just as negatively. A rich, resonant voice is a big benefit in business because it helps to convey power and confidence.

Practice exercise: Experiment with expression and meaning

A subtle change in punctuation can fundamentally change the meaning. Say each of these sentences aloud, noticing how you must change your stress, pause, and inflection to properly convey the idea.

Let's eat, mommy.
Let's eat mommy.

A woman, without her man, is nothing.
A woman: without her, man is nothing.

Call me fool if you wish.
Call me, fool, if you wish.

Ann Boleyn kept her head up defiantly an hour after she was beheaded.
Ann Boleyn kept her head up defiantly; an hour after, she was beheaded.

I want to thank my parents, the Pope and Mother Teresa.
I want to thank my parents, the Pope, and Mother Teresa.

The most influential of all vocal skills is resonance, which is the rumble or vibration in the voice. The more resonance in your voice, the more personal power you project. Some actors are iconic for their rich, rumbling voices. Depending on your generation, think Barry White, James Earl Jones, Seth MacFarlane, or Vin Diesel.

Nearly all actors and newscasters have resonant voices; it's a requirement of their trade. Actors use vocal resonance, or a lack thereof, as part of the overall composite to bring their characters to life. Royals, diplomats, military leaders, or high-powered executives are almost always portrayed with strong, powerful resonance. Characters with lesser status—the disempowered office worker, the undesirable blind date, the bumbling supervisor—are usually portrayed with weaker, higher-pitched, or strident voices.

Celebrities with strong resonant voices:

James Earl Jones
Angelina Jolie
Jeremy Irons
Antonio Banderas
Sigourney Weaver
Kelsey Grammer
Tom Brokaw
Oprah Winfrey
Meryl Streep
Morgan Freeman
Diane Sawyer
Robert Di Nero
Tommy Lee Jones
Allison Janney

Less-resonant voices are also deliberately used for comic effect, such as Pee Wee Herman, Edith Bunker, Gilbert Gottfried, Marge Simpson, and Fran Drescher. Especially in regard to women, we associate small voices with an image of sweetness, ditziness, or helplessness, such as Betty Boop, Minnie Mouse, or Marilyn Monroe. While these characters may be endearing, it's doubtful they'd be put in charge of a high-stakes contract in the business world.

A resonant voice will automatically inspire more confidence in your abilities. Have you ever had the experience of being on an airplane, and the pilot's voice over the intercom sounded wimpy, tired, or weak? Cognitively, we know the quality of a pilot's voice is not indicative of his or her piloting ability, but on a subliminal level a powerful voice will help us feel more confident that we'll arrive safely.

In general, men have bigger, more resonant voices than women. However, it's important to note this is more about socialization than physiology. The actual vocal mechanism that produces sound is the same in both genders, but because men are generally larger than women, their vocal mechanism is bigger. Just as in the difference between a viola and a violin, the size of the instrument does not dictate the power or richness of the sound.

We often "find our voices" in adolescence. As our bodies grow to adult size, our tones change, and we settle into our own unique sound. During adolescence, however, the social expectations and stereotypes for young men and women can be very different. The types of adjectives adolescent girls hope others might use to describe them are typically words such as *sweet, nice, thin,* or *petite,* and they may consciously or semiconsciously choose voices that represent those qualities. The kinds of adjectives adolescent boys hope others might use to describe them tend to be words like *big* and *strong,* so they often identify with voices representing those more powerful qualities.

As with so many communication skills, the way you produce your voice becomes habitual, but there's a big difference between habit and potential. If you aren't happy with the sound of your voice, you have the power to change it. Taking voice lessons from a professional vocal coach would be a great investment. As I mentioned earlier, most actors and news personalities have had some vocal training. And it doesn't have to be a lifelong commitment. As in working with a fitness trainer, once you know the exercises best suited for your personal issues, you can easily practice on your own.

In the meantime, a quick fix for bringing out more resonance in your voice is to increase your volume. When you speak at optimal volume, you are more likely to activate your diaphragm, and doing so is the first step toward developing resonance.

One trick I sometimes use to help someone connect to a more powerful voice is to ask him or her to imitate a Shakespearean actor. By "pretending" to have a booming voice, they do, in fact, produce one. They will often then say, "But that's not my real voice." If you can produce the sound, it belongs to you. Most people are fully capable of having rich, powerful voices but don't give themselves permission to do so. When coaching people on their singing voices, my friend Barbara will ask students to pretend they're opera singers. Bang! They immediately produce twice as much sound. For the opera singer and the Shakespearean actor, it's the same skill: engage your diaphragm. Flex your power by flexing your diaphragm.

Take a field trip to a networking meeting

One of the best places to practice your vocal skills is at networking meetings and conferences. At nearly every conference I've attended, at least 20 minutes are reserved for mingling. As you circulate around the room, there's one opportunity after another to practice vocal skills. Pick a skill like optimal volume or crisp articulation and give it full focus as you introduce yourself to other attendees. With the next person, try using pauses to slow down your pace. With a third person, test your expression. And with all, bring up the resonance. After all, the function of networking is to be noticed, so, literally, *let your voice be heard!*

Moving on

You've stayed with me through posture, hand and facial gestures, and the importance of a powerful voice. But we aren't done yet. Next we'll take a good "look" at the power of eye contact.

When it comes to credibility, *seeing* really is *believing!*

To watch a short video of the author
demonstrating the skills in this chapter,
scan the box above or
enter this URL into your browser.

www.thecredibilitycode.com/video/vcxm93

CHAPTER 4

Eye Contact:
Seeing Eye to Eye

"Eye contact is the best accessory."
– TAKAYUKI IKKAKU

A classic episode of the television program *Candid Camera* (1948–2004) shows how easy it is to look at people without really seeing them. In the gag, an actor poses as a customer service representative at a hardware store. As the "representative" speaks to an unsuspecting customer at the counter, two men carrying a large piece of plywood walk between them, temporarily blocking the customer's view of the representative. During this brief break, another actor replaces the first actor, standing in the same spot, wearing the same vest. The customers typically do not seem to notice the change, continuing the conversation as if the new representative were the original one.

As the gag continues, the changes between the representatives are increasingly exaggerated—different outfits, hairstyles, even genders—before customers start to react and thus draw even more laughs from the audience. This *Candid Camera* episode is humorous, but it also demonstrates the distinction between simply looking at someone and really *seeing* someone.

> ## Eye Contact Codes of Conduct
> • Hold eye contact for three to five seconds per person.
> • Engage everyone in the room.
> • Keep your focus up.
> • Be interactive.

In human interactions, eye contact is vital. Pedestrians won't step into the crosswalk until they've made clear eye contact with the driver coming to the intersection. Babies begin to track people with their eyes at about 8 to 12 weeks old. A certain look from a parent may bring a misbehaving child under control.

In the business world, we often assess people who make clear eye contact as being in control, focused, confident, and open. People of authority are often unwilling to begin speaking until all eyes are on them. People who avoid eye contact may be considered shy, evasive, distracted, or bored.

Have you ever heard someone say, "Can you look me in the eye and say that?" In the Western world, eye contact is a key indicator of credibility. It is not just *making* eye contact that creates credibility, however. It's *holding* eye contact. The duration of the eye contact matters.

Optimal duration for holding eye contact varies widely among different cultures. As with any behavior, it's a good idea to pay attention to the social norms of the culture you're encountering for clues as to what's appropriate. In the Western world, and especially the United States, holding eye contact for three to five seconds per person is considered optimal.

Optimal eye contact scale

Once again, however, there's a difference between being adequate and being optimal. Here's the evaluation scale that I use in my workshops:

1. **Absent**—Not looking at the listeners in any way: The speaker's eyes are on the floor or gazing into space.
2. **Below Average**—Scanning back and forth like a sprinkler system. While it's better than eyes on the floor or ceiling, the speaker is not truly seeing anyone.
3. **Adequate**—Holding for one to two seconds per person. While acceptable, the speaker is missing the opportunity to make a true connection with the listeners or read their signals.
4. **Optimal**—Holding for three to five seconds per person. The speaker sees the listeners as individuals, visually connecting with each one for a short time as if it were a one-on-one conversation.
5. **Too much**—Holding for more than five seconds per person. This is an absolute rarity; I've met fewer than 10 people in my lifetime who hold eye contact too long.

Eye contact is reciprocal

Human communication is a two-way street. If you smile at someone, they are likely to smile back. If you say "Hi," they are likely to say "Hi" back. The same is true for eye contact.

When the focus turns to you—whether it's around the conference room table or during a formal presentation—you're the leader in that moment. And as the leader, you set the standard for the kind of eye contact you want to receive. If you give your listeners strong eye contact, they are unconsciously obligated to give strong eye contact back to you. Your eye contact is a nonverbal invitation for them to pay attention to you. Yes, it's true that some people will ignore the invitation, just as some people may not feel obligated to return your smile. For the most part, however, if you offer strong eye contact, you are likely to receive it.

People in my workshops often tell me it's difficult to speak when everyone is looking at them. In reality, it's much more difficult to speak when people are *not* paying attention to you. Eye contact is reciprocal. If you speak and people aren't looking at you, your first question should be, "Am I looking at *them*?" As with so many skills in this book, it's within your power to entice others to communicate more effectively with you: If you pay more attention to them, they will pay more attention to you.

> *As with so many skills in this book, it's within your power to entice others to communicate more effectively with you. . . .*

Another complaint I often hear at my workshops is that participants find it distracting to talk and make eye contact at the same time. They say it's hard to think. While they may find it hard to think, the problem is usually not direct eye contact, per se. The problem is being *self-conscious* about the *eye contact*. I often ask if participants have the same difficulty in one-on-one conversations. "No," most reply. "One-on-one eye contact is not a problem."

Most of us process fairly well when we are absorbed in our job, focused on the task at hand. We become self-conscious and distracted when we focus on ourselves *performing* that task rather than just *doing* it. For example, we've all walked down the stairs thousands of times without giving it a thought because it's a subroutine performed over and over again. But try walking down a flight of stairs *consciously focusing on the mechanics of each step* and somehow we are more likely to trip up.

We maintain better eye contact in one-on-one communication because we're not conscious of doing so. We move through our day, holding one-on-one eye contact for 10 to 15 seconds at a stretch, having hundreds of individual eye contact interactions without once giving them a conscious thought.

To avoid becoming distracted by eye contact in a group, practice it more often so that it becomes an *unconscious subroutine, just like descending the steps in a staircase.* Work hard to make strong eye contact a habit so that it no longer takes conscious (or self-conscious) effort.

Case Study: Nikhil eyes the issue

As a software engineer, Nikhil's daily life is steeped in logic and process. Most of his interactions involve a keyboard and monitor. But he is often called upon to explain his technology to potential corporate clients. Paired with a representative from the sales department, Nikhil must then convince prospects that his software is the right stuff to drive their project. However, even though Nikhil is the mastermind behind the software, the sales department began to complain that his presence in prospect meetings was actually detrimental to gaining new business. He looked bored, evasive, and uncommitted. Nikhil's issue? He simply couldn't make eye contact.

When I met with Nikhil, he said he wasn't trying to be uncooperative, but eye contact made him extremely uncomfortable. Somewhere along the way, he said, making eye contact was so uncomfortable he just gave up trying. And in fact, he didn't understand what the big fuss was about. If he didn't like it, why did he have to do it?

I told him it may not be the way *he* functions best in the world, but the greater portion of the population finds eye contact vital for understanding and connection. And, while it is possible to be competent in one's area of expertise without this skill, eventually it could become a disadvantage. At some point in his career, I warned, his lack of eye contact would hold him back from reaching his greatest potential.

To make my point on his turf, I revealed one of my own failings. "I'm somewhat of a technophobe," I confessed. "Imagine if I told you I refuse to use computers because they make me uncomfortable. You'd likely tell me, like it or not, computers are a reality of how the world does business." He got the point.

So we set to work. I started by having him answer impromptu questions while keeping his eyes glued to a Post-it note at eye level across from him. Just by keeping his eyes up, he looked significantly more engaged. Then I sat where the Post-it note had been. At first, his eyes darted away from me repeatedly, and I simply gave him a gentle reminder to focus back on me. Within 20 minutes, he could stay with me continuously.

Granted, this wasn't true eye contact; he had just become desensitized to looking at me. To make it feel more natural, I introduced some new ground rules. He could let his eyes drift away from me briefly, as long as 1) his eyes stayed at eye level (no looking down) and 2) each time he looked at me, he stayed for a minimum of three seconds (no darting). He found this suggestion a big relief and eagerly took it on. I then recruited a couple of his most trusted officemates to sit in with us. Within 90 minutes from the time we started, he was holding eye contact comfortably with all of us. To keep his progress moving forward, I instructed him to practice the above drill with his colleagues for 10 minutes a day for three weeks. When I followed up with Nikhil a few weeks later, he reported that he and his sales staff were finding their client visits much more productive and enjoyable.

Reading signals

A person who makes strong eye contact can better read other people's nonverbal signals. Have you ever heard the phrase "read your audience"? Eye contact is how it takes place: You have to really *see* them to *read* them.

In casual one-on-one communication, we're constantly reading the signals of the listener to look for clues as to how our message is being absorbed and accepted. If the listener looks confused, we go into more detail. If we sense impatience, we move ahead more quickly. If someone looks skeptical, we seek to clarify any questions. We change the flavor and flow of our sentences based on the listener's nonverbal hints. It's a win-win situation for both parties: We feel more comfortable and attuned to what we need to say next, and the listener gets his or her needs met more efficiently.

However, during our highest stakes conversations—a million-dollar client proposal or a vital meeting with the board of directors—we often forget to use these valuable skills. We become so consumed with what we need to say and do that we become overly *self*-focused. It's very difficult to observe another person's signals when you are mentally watching your own.

The solution, again, is eye contact. When you gain the discipline of holding eye contact for three to five seconds per person, you will automatically turn your focus back to them.

Eye contact and nervousness

In my workshops, participants often joke that the longest journey in the world is from their chair to that vast open space at the front of the room. They can go from relaxed and comfortable to jittery and scatter-brained in less than five feet. It's dismaying what happens to our internal chemistry when we are thrust into the spotlight. Nervousness is hardwired into all of us. It's a very human, albeit primitive, reaction. Why would standing in front of 10 friendly, supportive people produce so much angst and adrenaline?

Imagine you are a creature in the woods and 10 sets of eyes are silently staring at you. What would that mean for you? "Am I prey? Am I about to be eaten?" Your primitive brain, that part of you watching for dangerous situations, finds it threatening to be at the front of the room. You are singled out from the crowd with a sea of silent, expressionless faces focused intently on you. It's very unsettling.

Such a reaction doesn't just happen in front of large groups. If you're sitting in a hotel lobby and *one* person—motionless, expressionless—is continuously staring at you, you'll find it unnerving. We simply don't like to be stared at.

One of the defensive things your primitive brain tells you to do is to dart your eyes around. If you were in a truly dangerous spot, you would dart your eyes around to keep track of all dangers, right? Nervousness and darting eyes are very closely associated; they are a key signal used to assess nervousness in others. But perhaps most important for this discussion, darting your eyes has a profound impact on your thought process.

Practice exercise: Focus your thoughts

Take a moment to read the next three sentences and then try the exercise on your own. Wherever you are, dart your eyes from one spot to another. Then, with your eyes still skipping about, try to verbalize directions from your house to your favorite grocery store. Keep your eyes moving the whole time: Start now.

How was your thought process? Was it scattered? Most people find it extremely difficult to think and dart their eyes around at the same time. Even if we felt perfectly prepared before talking, we suddenly can't put a coherent sentence together. It's amazing, but if you dart your eyes around for a full minute, you can significantly raise the level of adrenaline in your system. It not only perpetuates the feeling of being nervous: it can even create it.

In workshops, the video camera allows us to go back and analyze what's really going on in those first few moments when participants introduce themselves at the front of the room. Invariably, the speaker's eyes are flitting around.

But you can take control over the unconscious eye-darting habit. You have to overcome some primitive wiring, but you can train yourself to keep your eyes still when you're under pressure. By focusing your eyes on individual listeners, you effectively halt that panicky physiological response. You'll have the outward appearance of being calm and self-controlled, and you will process your thoughts more effectively.

What's the vital takeaway here? When you focus your eyes, you focus your thoughts.

EYE CONTACT CODE #1
Hold eye contact for three to five seconds per person

After listening to thousands of workshop participants, I know you're thinking: "Really? Three to five seconds per person? Isn't that way too long?" Here's the honest answer. Yes, but only if you were to stare zombie-like at individuals for three to five seconds. Then it might come across as too intense or even creepy. But as long as your facial gestures stay naturally animated, three to five seconds per person feels conversational and relaxed.

We play a game in my workshops that gives the participants a trustworthy version of what this rhythm really feels and looks like. As one participant talks at the front of the room for a minute or two, I have everyone else raise one hand. It's the speaker's job to get everyone's hand down, one by one, by looking at them for three to five seconds. The listeners are instructed to count off the seconds and lower their hands somewhere between three and five seconds. After watching an entire classroom of participants do this drill, even the most resistant of students will admit that three to five seconds looks the most relaxed and natural.

I know you can't count off the seconds in your head, murmuring to yourself "one-thousand one, one-thousand two, one-thousand three." Your brain is obviously too busy for that. To create the rhythm of three to five seconds on your own, try speaking one thought or phrase to one person, and when you reach the comma or the pause, turn and give the next thought or phrase to someone else. In short, *let the structure of your sentences* guide your rhythm.

Even in one-on-one conversations, your goal is to hold eye contact for a minimum of three to five seconds. Most of us easily hold eye contact for 10, 15, even 30 seconds at a stretch in individual conversations. However, occasionally we become self-conscious of our one-on-one eye contact and begin to think, "Wow, I've been looking at you for a long time. This is weird . . . should I look away?"

The good news is that it's okay to look away. However, two rules apply:

1. If you look away, you must come back. And each time you come back, you must hold eye contact for a minimum of three to five seconds.

2. Your eyes should stay on the horizon. Feel free to take your gaze to the side but keep your head and eyes level. Don't look down at your papers or up at the ceiling.

A note about using notes: It's okay to look down at your notes. I'm an advocate of notes; they keep us focused on the message, and, without them, we can forget important points or take unwanted tangents. Feel free to use them and look at them when you need them. But important ground rules apply to using notes: First, they should be bullet points no more than seven words long. Fully written-out sentences are not notes; they are scripts. Reading from a script is not only deadly boring to your listener, but it lowers your credibility by making you look like you don't own the information. Second, if your mouth is moving, your eyes should be on your listener. That means that if you need to look at your notes, pause briefly and look. Pausing is good and as long is there is no apology in your body language, your listeners will comfortably wait for you.

EYE CONTACT CODE #2
Engage everyone in the room

When speaking to a group, I encourage people to use the sheepdog technique of constantly corralling the wandering sheep. Similarly, a speaker needs to round up the audience. Never let any part of the room go too long without some attention from you. Maintain a wide, random sweep, avoiding any observable pattern.

And try not to play favorites. Too many speakers make the mistake of looking only at the leaders or decision makers in the room or of spending a disproportionate amount of time engaged with the active listeners. Maintain eye contact with everyone, regardless of rank or apparent enthusiasm. You'll seem more like a leader, more inclusive, and more in command.

In larger groups, you may not be able to look at everyone; try to make eye contact with each section of the room. Envision the room as the "five" side on a die—four black corner dots and one center dot. Develop a pattern of randomly checking each dot in the room, holding three to five seconds with each section. This is far more effective than the sprinkler system version of eye contact of rhythmically sweeping back and forth, not really seeing anyone.

EYE CONTACT CODE #3
Keep your focus up

I'm sure you've seen this pattern before: The speaker talks to the audience for a phrase or two, then to the floor for a phrase or two, back to the audience, then the floor, audience, floor, audience, floor.

Imagine a baseball outfielder who consistently drifts his attention away from the diamond to gaze at the grass in front of him. Would you feel he was "in the game?"

When you drop eye contact, you're dropping out of the game. The energy in the room drops, too. *Remember: Communication is reciprocal.* If you expect your audience to pay attention to you the entire time, you need to pay attention to them the entire time. Give your listeners the respect you expect from them—your full attention.

I realize that sometimes you need to gather your thoughts. In these moments, it's all right to move your eyes to the side for a few seconds and find your wording. But the same rule applies as with using notes: If your mouth is moving, your eyes should be on your listeners.

Make it a habit to keep your head level and your eyes on the horizon at all times, even when you are listening. You'll look more attentive, energized, and respectful.

Practice exercise: Grab some Post-it notes

Part of developing effective eye contact is learning the choreography and rhythm of looking around the room and holding eye contact for three to five seconds. This exercise can be done standing or seated.

Put blank Post-it notes on the walls of your office or living room. Give yourself an impromptu question and hold your eyes for three to five seconds on each note while answering. Let your sentence structure be your cue to move from note to note. When you reach a comma or a pause in the idea, move to another note. Try not to follow a set pattern and practice engaging the entire room. Even after you've mastered this exercise, it's still helpful when preparing for an upcoming high-stakes presentation. Instead of just memorizing your material, you'll have practiced how to *deliver* it.

EYE CONTACT CODE #4
Be interactive

It's not enough to simply look at your listeners; you must truly engage with them. While three to five seconds per person is an appropriate pace, it's not about robotically moving from one person to another as if shooting little bobbing wooden ducks at the state fair. You must *interact*. Your face, hands, and voice must be expressive: Each time you turn your focus to another person, acknowledge them. Nodding, raising your eyebrows, smiling, and "reaching out" with your gestures are effective ways to let your listeners know it's a conversation, not a lecture.

> *Nodding, raising your eyebrows, smiling, and "reaching out" with your gestures are effective ways to let your listeners know it's a conversation, not a lecture.*

While it's helpful to follow a few technical ground rules, the key to effective eye contact is connection to your listeners. You must truly *see* them, and they need to *know* that you see them. This is the human part of the equation in eye contact, and we'll take a deeper dive into this idea in chapter 6, Focus: Making a Connection.

Take a field trip to a restaurant

Gather a group of friends together for a nice dinner out to focus on your eye contact skills. Your friends don't need to know this is your objective, but it's a perfect low-risk situation to give this skill some attention. A group of four to six is just the right size: large enough to practice, but small enough so people won't pair up into smaller conversations. If possible, arrange to sit at a round table so that everyone can easily look at everyone else. During the meal, try to work in a story or two about your day or some adventure you've taken, all the while keeping your eyes on their eyes. Even when listening, focus your eyes on whoever is speaking.

You don't have to wait for a special event to practice this; if you typically have meals with family or colleagues, you already have practice opportunities built into your regular routine.

Moving on

So far we've addressed the need to have a strong posture, a strong voice, and strong eye contact. These are the three pillars that hold up your appearance of credibility. Learning these behaviors should be at the top of your "to do" list. But let's not forget about those behaviors that you shouldn't do? As you'll see in chapter 5, it's all too often the behaviors to which we are most blind that derail our appearance of credibility and confidence.

To watch a short video of the author
demonstrating the skills in this chapter,
scan the box above or
enter this URL into your browser.

www.thecredibilitycode.com/video/erpt72

The Derailers:
Cleaning up Your Act

*"There are always three speeches for every one you actually gave.
The one you practiced, the one you gave,
and the one you wish you gave."*

– DALE CARNEGIE

Perhaps you've seen this video experiment. Six people, three wearing black shirts and three wearing white shirts, are tossing around two basketballs. The viewer is asked to count how many times the white-shirted players pass the ball. When the video stops, the correct answer is displayed: Fifteen. Then the viewer is asked a startling question: Did you see the gorilla? It's amazing, but only about half of all viewers typically notice the man in the gorilla suit. When viewed a second time, it's astounding that he could be missed at all. He strolls directly through the center of the players, even taking a moment to turn toward the camera and pound his chest. See for yourself; watch the video at www.invisiblegorilla.com. This and other experiments in selective attentiveness are outlined in *The Invisible Gorilla*, a book by Christopher Chabris and Daniel Simons.

When communicating face-to-face, most people have lots of little gorillas wandering through their conversations in the form of extraneous filler words or excessive fidgeting. If your listeners are intently focused on your message, they may not notice these distractions. But if the listeners' attention is drawn to the distractions, these seemingly small behaviors can become the proverbial 800-pound gorilla in the room. That's why I call them "derailers."

An expert on leadership once told me it's not the big things that undermine the success of top executives. Rather, it's the accumulation of minor failings, such as not being on time, not keeping promises, not saying "thank you" . . . or simply distracting habits. This is even true for those who have a privileged background and an Ivy League education.

Caroline Kennedy, President John F. Kennedy's daughter, is a successful lawyer and author in her own right. When Hillary Clinton vacated her New York senate seat, Kennedy announced she was seeking the position. During an interview with *The New York Times* reporters Nicholas Confessore and David M. Halbfinger, they asked why she decided to run. Kennedy replied: "Um, this is a fairly unique moment both in our, you know, in our country's history, and, and in, in, you know, my own life, and, um, you know, we are facing, you know, unbelievable challenges, our economy, you know, health care, people are losing their jobs here in New York obviously, um, ah, you know."

Kennedy said, "you know" 12 times in less than a minute and 138 times during the entire interview. The next day, talk show hosts and media commentators pounced: She was the top story on the news but not for the reason she had hoped. Despite her high status, her campaign train was derailed by filler words.

It's a paradox: Our distracting behaviors aren't distracting to us. We are typically oblivious to them, and convincing people they are blind to their own bad habits is very difficult. Without video proof, it would be hard to convince someone who had *not* seen the gorilla that it walked directly through the basketball game. You'd face quite an argument.

The first step to cleaning up your communication style is to get some trustworthy feedback. When it comes to derailers, there's simply no substitute for the video camera. Try to capture a 10-minute clip of yourself in a typical business setting. Then, with the eye of a social scientist, examine the extraneous signals in your communication.

Remember that it's a matter of degrees; saying "you know" once in the course of a paragraph or occasionally shifting your position in your chair is not going to lower your credibility. Exhibiting these behaviors two or three times within a single sentence sends an entirely different message. The speaker who can eliminate the extra distractions from the conversation will automatically sound clearer, more focused, and better spoken.

Although there are hundreds of ways to distract your listeners, this chapter focuses on the four most common distracting behaviors that undercut credibility: using filler words, ending phrases with misplaced upward inflections, extraneous body movement, and "self-commenting." (Self-commenting is the act of conspicuously apologizing for verbal fumbles and mistakes.) Nearly all of my workshop participants need to work on at least one of these issues.

Derailer Codes of Conduct

• **Eliminate fillers.**
• **Avoid misplaced upward vocal inflections.**
• **Avoid extraneous movement.**
• **Eliminate self-commenting.**

DERAILER CODE #1
Eliminate fillers

Fillers are any words or sounds in your speech that are superfluous. In other words, when fillers are removed from the script, the message remains the same. What changes is the mood. Fillers often take the form of "uh," "ahhh," "um," or "ur." Sometimes fillers are actual words or phrases such as "you know," "kind of," "sort of," "actually," "basically," "right," "I mean," "okay," and "like." Even "and" and "so" can be fillers if we overuse them.

I once worked with a dynamic young CEO who had many positive attributes. He ran an innovative start-up business and had great people and great ideas. But here's an actual transcript of a speech he gave to launch his new technology. "So, I actually sort of passionately believe that we have an opportunity to, uh, you know, sort of really take this platform to a new level. So we just kind of, uh, need to jump in, you know, full force." He was trying to fire up his team and motivate them to succeed, but his language unintentionally softened his message into mush.

Imagine this same dynamic CEO saying, "I passionately believe we have the opportunity to take this platform to a new level. We need to jump in full force." This is articulate and concise and sends a more powerful message about the CEO's commitment.

Fillers include: uh, um, you know, kind of, actually, basically, I mean, right, okay, like.

Such oral habits are pervasive in our culture and four out of five people who come to my workshops use fillers excessively. And of those people who don't, many confess they've already worked on the problem. Unfortunately, you can't always rely on feedback from your friends, loved ones, or even colleagues concerning this behavior. If you have the filler habit, those people closest to you have most likely unconsciously filtered out your fillers, or they wouldn't be able to communicate with you. The only trustworthy feedback is video feedback.

Practice exercise: Record your habits

Record yourself the next time you are in a small-group meeting or record your end of an important telephone conversation. Play back a 10-minute segment and count your fillers. If you have more than one or two "uhs" and "ums" per paragraph, that's too many. If you use the same filler word more than a couple of times in the conversation, that's too often.

Note that fillers are especially prevalent when we are distracted, as when we are thinking on our feet or feeling nervous. These *are exactly the moments when it would be helpful to appear more self-assured.* For a true test, have a friend capture a few minutes of you speaking when you aren't aware that you're being recorded. We tend to be on our best behavior when we know we are being videotaped.

The tactical pause

Even when people know they have the filler-word habit, they tend to retain the problem because they don't know how to correct it. The solution is to pause; instead of interjecting that "um" or filler word, simply pause while your mind searches for the next word.

Most people develop the filler habit because they are uncomfortable with pausing. Do not fear the pause; great speakers have made effective tactical use of pausing for emphasis and to elicit audience reaction. Dr. Martin Luther King Jr. was a master at it. Search out a recording of his 1963 "I Have a Dream" speech or his talk in a Memphis church the night before his assassination. His connection with his audience was electric, and he took full advantage of this voltage.

Practice exercise: "The Flag Game"

Sit across from a partner and take turns answering robust questions like those below. Use a stopwatch and spend at least two minutes on each answer:
- What are your favorite movies, books, or travel destinations?
- What are five things you like about your occupation?
- If you won the lottery, how would you invest or spend the money?
- What possession(s) would you keep if all else were lost?
- If you could, what big change would you make in your life?

While you are speaking, have your partner "flag," (briefly raise a hand) each time you use a filler phrase or word. Although I would never give this instruction in any other setting, it's important your partner ignore your answers and listen *solely for your filler words*. As the speaker, try not to react to your partner's flags. Just notice the flag in the back of your mind and keep talking.

Speaking for a full two minutes is important because it can be challenging to talk that long. You'll probably have moments when you're searching for what to say next and *that's exactly when the "uhs" and "ums" tend to creep into your message.*

Prescription for success

Here's the prescription for successfully eliminating your fillers for the long term. Make a chart with 20 check boxes waiting to be filled in. Play the flag game 20 times in the next two weeks. At first, it will take a great deal of your concentration to pull out the fillers. But in fewer than 10 practice sessions, most people will consistently be able to complete a two-minute impromptu conversation without fillers! You must do the drill the full 20 times, however. It's like taking antibiotics: Even if you're feeling better, you must complete the full course. In the long run, you aren't really learning how to eliminate fillers; you're learning how to pause while you think instead of using fillers.

> *What if Caroline Kennedy, with her legendary brand identity, had played the flag game with her advisors two weeks prior to all those interviews? She might be a U.S. senator right now.*

If you aren't seeing significant improvement after five practice sessions, you may have to increase the pain level a bit: Start paying your partner for every "uh" or "um" he or she catches. Be creative. Pay in cash or desserts or turns doing the dishes—whatever will keep you motivated. What if Caroline Kennedy, with her legendary brand identity, had played the flag game with her advisors two weeks prior to all those interviews? She might be a U.S. senator right now.

Learning and implementing many of the skills in this book can make it easy to become "consciously competent." We can almost instantly increase our volume or stand up straight if we ask ourselves to. Yet even when giving it conscious effort, many people find it difficult to drop the fillers from their speech . . . at first. However, with intentional practice, the learning curve for this skill does not have to be very long.

Practice exercise: Talk to yourself

Once you have some control over your fillers, practice by talking to yourself. While driving alone in your car or cooking or walking the dog, give yourself an impromptu question and concentrate on eliminating fillers. Practice your 30-second elevator pitch of who you are and what you do. Introducing yourself should not be an impromptu exercise. We all do it hundreds of times, so make sure your introduction is free of "uhs" and "ums."

Test your skills when you leave phone messages. Most phone systems will allow you to listen to your message and re-record it if you hit the star key. Make a promise to yourself never to leave another phone message that contains a filler.

DERAILER CODE #2
Avoid misplaced upward vocal inflections

Misplaced upward inflections, also called "up talk," can be defined as an upward inflection? that sounds like a question mark? at the end of your sentence? It can give the impression? that you're seeking approval? or you aren't as committed? or as mature? as you might like to come across? Am I making sense?

Everyone knows someone who speaks this way.

The "valley girl" accent

One of the characters in the movie *American Pie* (1999) begins every story with, "One time? at band camp?" The film intentionally mocks this vocal pattern, but many young adults don't recognize the satire because this inflection is now so common.

If you were an adult in the 1980s when the "valley girls" first began to speak this way, you probably found it unusual if not comical. But succeeding generations have grown up in a culture in which this speech pattern is commonplace. They don't necessarily regard misplaced upward inflections as detrimental to their credibility. When I work with high-tech companies employing many smart young people, they will even ask, "What's wrong with that pattern?" or "Why would I need to change it?" In fact, they hear the pattern as a way of being inviting or collaborative. To them the nonverbal function of the upward inflection is to say, "Does this make sense to you?"

If the younger workforce interacted only with their peers, this upward vocal pattern might not jeopardize their credibility. But many people in the older generation—*need I say, people in the role of employers, investors, or corporate business partners*—perceive the inflection as a lack of self-assuredness or maturity.

Imagine that you are the employer interviewing a potential candidate who says, "I believe I'm the right person for this job? You can count on me?" Would you find that tone of voice reassuring?

Unfortunately this vocal pattern is contagious. We take on the style and patterns of the people we interact with everyday, and if you enter a new work environment in which many people end statements with upward inflections, it's likely you'll unconsciously pick up the same pattern.

In my early years as a coach, people would often refer to this vocal pattern as the California accent. However, in the last couple of decades, I've witnessed this inflection work its way across the United States, first becoming prevalent on the coasts and then filling in the Midwest. Now I'm increasingly hearing it in Europe. It's possible that this inflection will someday become so pervasive that it will fall off the derailer list. But that's not happened yet, so focus on today, not someday. You have nothing to lose and everything to gain by taking control of this bad habit.

Start high and end low

Before the 1980s, the typical phrasing of the American English accent started high and ended low. Declarative statements required a downward inflection that began at a mid to high pitch and cascaded downward to a low pitch.

Upward inflections at the ends of phrases had one of two functions: To indicate a question or indicate a list. When listing, the inflection implies there is more to follow. You might say, "I'm going to the grocery store to get apples (upward inflection), butter (upward inflection), and juice (downward inflection)."

> *If you'd like to eliminate your misplaced upward inflections, start the correction at the beginning of the sentence.*

But the valley girls were true rebels. They intentionally created an accent that was the exact opposite of the traditional speech pattern. They used upward inflections to make declarative statements: They started low and ended high.

If you'd like to eliminate your misplaced upward inflections, start the correction at the beginning of the sentence. Start high and end low.

Practice exercise: Make a strong statement

I hear the upward inflection pattern most prominently in introductions, when the speaker is welcoming the audience and stating his or her credentials. Take a moment right now to write out your credentials: your name, department, job title, how long you've been with the company, and the vital role you play. Now practice saying all this logistical information with a confident, downward inflection. Intentionally begin each statement at a fairly high pitch and end each phrase at a low pitch.

Practice exercise: Retrain your ear

To take control of your inflections, you'll need to distinguish the difference between an upward inflection and a downward inflection.

1. **Exaggerate your inflections:** Say the following words out loud three times using a *rising* inflection, as if you are asking a question. Start each word or phrase at the same pitch but try to make the rise in inflection greater each time.
   - Who?
   - Now?
   - Me?
   - Is this yours?

Say the following words out loud three times using a downward inflection, as if you are firmly giving an instruction. Exaggerate the downward inflection each time, making sure to start each word or phrase at the same pitch.
   - No!
   - You!
   - Over there!
   - Try again!
   - Yes, I can!

2. **Isolate sentences:** Now practice on random words. Look around the room and identify what you see using a downward inflection: book, computer, telephone. Put each word at the end of a sentence. "I like this book." "This is my computer." "I have to answer the telephone."

Take a field trip to your living room

If you're not sure what that high-to-low cascade sounds like, turn on the TV and scrutinize the vocal pattern of a national newscaster. Since it's true that many newscasters sound phony or pretentious, choose someone you find credible and authentic. Repeat his or her words, mimicking the vocal pattern. Then pick up the newspaper and read a story out loud trying to use the same pattern.

DERAILER CODE #3
Avoid extraneous movements

One of the biggest derailers of confident behavior is extraneous movement: fidgeting, changing your position in your chair, shifting your weight, or head bobbing. If you do these things only once or twice in the course of a conversation, it's not a credibility breaker. The issue is frequency.

In general, being still raises your status by demonstrating that you are in a state of control, not a state of distraction.

People rarely do these behaviors intentionally. However, it's the very fact that these behaviors are unintentional that creates the impression the speaker lacks self-awareness or self-control. In general, being still raises your status by demonstrating that you are in a state of control, not a state of distraction.

How his body worked against him

During a group workshop at an architectural firm, one of the project leaders stepped to the front of the room to practice introducing himself. During the few minutes he spoke, he shifted his weight back and forth, repositioned his feet, and bobbed his head. The company's director of business development had been observing the workshop to see how his team was performing. Later he confided to me, "Wow, if this is how he introduces himself to new clients, I've got to wonder how much business we've lost. If he can't manage his body, how can he be expected to manage a project?"

It would be unfortunate to be passed over for a project simply because you haven't learned how to stand still. As judgmental or unfair as this sounds, hiring is as much subliminal and emotional as it is logical and procedural. I recall a hiring manager at a high tech company, a place filled with logical thinkers, once saying, "My gut tells me that I don't want to hire this guy. I just haven't figured out why. He looks so . . . *unsettled.*"

Here are some of the extraneous movements that diminish your personal power:

- Swaying or shifting weight from hip to hip
- Jiggling one knee or shaking a leg
- Rocking back and forth on your heels
- Popping or bending your knees
- Repositioning your feet as if you're trying to find your footing
- Fiddling with rings or pens
- Twisting or swinging the upper body
- Tapping fingers or toes
- Shrugging one or both shoulders
- Flopping hands down and slapping legs
- Bobbing your head or excessive nodding
- Wandering around while speaking

In my workshops, people often say, "I just can't be still. I can't help myself." They may even believe that their extraneous movements help them manage stress. The truth is that such behaviors are symptoms of stress and only feel good because they are ingrained habits.

After coaching thousands of people, I can offer you a solid promise: If you eliminate these behaviors, you'll not only look more comfortable, you'll feel more comfortable. After a very short learning curve, nearly everyone I work with reports they feel more grounded, more focused, and more powerful when they are still. It's worth the effort to practice this at every opportunity, not just at big meetings and events.

> **Practice exercise: Knock your socks off**
>
> One trick an actor will use to make a character look flighty or scatter-brained is to move his or her head like a bobblehead doll. Excessive head movement may help you look enthusiastic, but it can also chip away at your credibility.
>
> If you move your head too much when you talk, practice holding it still. Fold a thick pair of socks, balance them on your head, and try to talk for several minutes without the socks falling off. You should be able to look easily around the room, but if your head bobbles or tilts, the socks will likely drop. Don't forget that your head should move independently of your shoulders; your nose and eyes need to point in the same direction. The trick is to stay animated with your face and hands while keeping your head level.

DERAILER CODE #4
Eliminate self-commenting

It happens to all of us: We mispronounce a word and then correct it. We use faulty grammar and fix it. We start a sentence one way and then restart it with different words. In casual conversation, we fumble our words once or twice in each paragraph. We instantly and automatically correct these little mistakes; it's a natural communication subroutine.

But when we feel self-conscious, as in a high stakes meeting or a formal presentation, we begin to notice and react to every *little mistake we make.* If we trip over a word, we may verbally apologize with a quick "I'm sorry." Or worse, we may feel compelled to joke by saying something silly, such as "Gee there's something wrong with my mouth today," or "I just haven't had enough coffee yet."

If not a verbal apology, we resort to a nonverbal reflex, such as wincing, crinkling our noses, shaking our heads, rolling our eyes, smiling apologetically, or shrugging our shoulders. Ouch!

I call this "self-commenting." And unfortunately, fumbling on our fumbles only aggravates the problem. Mispronouncing a word and then correcting it is not the issue: The derailer is *your visible preoccupation with it.* Never let your listener see or hear your internal self-evaluation of how you are doing. Mistakes happen: Simply correct them and move on.

Habitual apologies

In Japanese, the Kanji symbol for flinching or the act of self-commenting translates directly to "facial apology." People often use a verbal or facial apology to deflect criticism. Sometimes these behaviors become deeply ingrained habits.

Kimi was very deferential. Whenever she made the slightest mistake, she would say, "I'm sorry" or "Excuse me." Every time I gave her an instruction during on-camera coaching, such as "Try balancing your weight over both feet" or "Try lifting your chin," she would whisper an apology while making the adjustment. Worse, when I pointed out such apologies, she apologized for apologizing.

To correct the problem, I began using the American Sign Language sign for "sorry" whenever I saw the behavior, with the instruction she should not react to my signal in any way. For a few minutes, she winced every time I flashed the sign, but soon she was able to accept my corrections with her face relaxed and her head up. The ability to accept feedback with your head level and eyes forward shows a great deal of personal confidence.

Be like a duck on water

Imagine a duck moving quickly across a pond. On the surface, the duck is effortlessly gliding along, but underneath, its two feet are paddling vigorously.

When thinking on your feet, it's an art to look like you're gliding when inside you're paddling. However, sometimes when we are struggling as speakers, we give the listener a running commentary of our inner process. "Oh, I've lost my train of thought . . . what's that word? Oh, I'm taking so long. . . . It's right on the tip of my . . . eeerrr, how embarrassing . . . My mind's a blank . . . this is so frustrating!" By describing how hard we are working, we feel we might somehow get credit for all of the effort. But this is just another form of self-commenting. In the long run, it's more empowering to keep this information to yourself. Wouldn't you rather look like the person who effortlessly handles difficult situations?

Practice exercise: Play with words

Fictionary is a great game to help you eliminate the impulse to self-comment. Ask a partner to give you a gibberish word—any string of syllables arbitrarily put together. Repeat the word aloud and then define it, as if you've known the word all of your life. It's likely your brain will give you push back at some point by saying, "This isn't very good," or "I'm really messing this up." The game can help you practice the discipline of ignoring your internal criticism.

How do you win this game? By looking like an expert! Since you're defining a gibberish word, there's no correct answer. Your goal is to look confident, even though your brain is "paddling." Don't show any "tells"—that poker term for giving away your hand. If you give your listener any verbal or nonverbal indication of your discomfort, you lose. Practice this skill in low-risk situations so you can pull it off when it matters.

Tail wagging

Dogs will often meet perceived aggression with low-status tail wagging. When confronted by a more dominant dog, a timid dog will wag its tail, lower its posture, or even roll over on its back to expose its belly, saying "No contest. Here are my abdominal viscera. You can chew me up." The dominant dog acknowledges this submissive behavior by backing off, as if to say, "Okay, I don't have to kill you as long as you know I'm in charge." Such humiliating behavior works for the low-status dog that wants to survive.

When confronted with threatening situations, such as being thrust into the spotlight in a high-stakes meeting, humans often behave in similar ways. We don't roll over and show our bellies, but we roll our hands inwardly to show the underside of our palms and forearms, shuffle our feet, dip our chins, lower our eyes, tilt our heads, and/or concave our shoulders to diminish our posture. We may even smile sheepishly.

It's the human version of tail wagging. We're essentially saying, "Don't hurt me. I submit." Listeners may feel sympathy, they may even find you endearing, but you'll lose credibility and the listeners' respect even as they reflexively smile back. It's just another form of self-commenting by letting the listener see your internal self-doubt.

Most people are familiar with the "fight-or-flight" response, the rush of adrenalin that prepares us either to fight or to run for our lives when we feel threatened. Though not as well known, there's a second chemical at work in our bodies when we are under stress: oxytocin. Oxytocin is the "relationship chemical." When it's released under stress, it produces the "tend-and-befriend" response. Instead of fighting or fleeing, we employ another tactic: Make friends with the enemy.

The feminine version of tail wagging can look like timid flirting. It might include the flash of a smile, chin down, eyebrows raised, eyes dropping to the floor, shoulders tilted. The nonverbal subtext sends the message that one is either so meek or so nice that no one would dream of hurting her. "Please take it easy on me. I'm really uncomfortable on the spot."

The masculine version of tail wagging looks like shy indifference. The posture is extremely casual—weight leaning to the side, head down, hands behind the back or in the pockets, archetypically kicking the dirt and saying, "Shucks, gee whiz." The nonverbal subtext is non-threatening because it's clear he's not going to fight for his position. "Whatever. I can take it or leave it."

Both men and women display both the feminine and masculine versions of tail wagging. And it's a common tactic . . . *because it works.* If you exhibit this low-status behavior, other people typically respond by backing off. In essence, you're asking your listeners to lower the bar for you. They respectfully comply by *lowering their expectations of you* as well. They may even write you off completely.

While this behavior is driven by automatic-pilot responses meant to protect us under stress, we can counteract this response. The solution is strong posture, strong voice, and strong eye contact.

Take a field trip to a trade show or job fair

Trade shows, conferences, and job fairs are great places for you to work on any of the skills discussed in this book. Farmers' markets and festivals can provide a low-risk practice opportunity. Any place with exhibits and people in booths will do.

It's customary in these environments to step up to strangers and start chatting. At each booth, focus on a different skill. Start by exhibiting strong posture, a strong voice, and strong eye contact. Avoid fidgeting, even when you're listening, and use a strong declarative inflection when stating who you are and what you do. See if you can get through the entire day without self-commenting, apologizing, or tail wagging. And don't forget to be attentive to the filler words in your communication.

Sometimes these events can be career-building opportunities. If you are the candidate at a job fair, each person you meet has the potential to influence your future. If you are the exhibitor at a trade show, a business prospect might walk right up to you. At bigger trade shows, top executives are often mingling with the crowd, giving you rare access to introduce yourself. Prepare yourself for these opportunities by getting the derailers out of your communication before you arrive.

Moving on

So far we've focused on what *you* need to do to appear confident and credible. But there is another vital component to every conversation: *them*. It's not enough to look good if you're not creating a relationship with your listener. To truly raise the bar in your communication, you'll need to learn how make a connection.

To watch a short video of the author
demonstrating the skills in this chapter,
scan the box above or
enter this URL into your browser.

www.thecredibilitycode.com/video/dyna38

CHAPTER 6

Focus:
Making a Connection

"Never treat your audience as customers, always as partners."
— JAMES STEWART

A seeing-eye dog provides an elite class of service. Training begins in the first few weeks of puppyhood and includes learning impeccable house manners and obedience skills. If it makes the cut into formal guide-dog training, the dog must learn to stay focused on the job at all times and ignore those things that might naturally distract it, such as squirrels, balls, over-zealous children, or a discarded chicken bone. And finally, the dog learns to look for obstacles from the human point of view, such as a low-hanging branch or a two-by-four jutting out the back of a pickup truck. This is no small feat for an animal that normally keeps its nose to the ground.

Yet even after all of this rigorous training, the dog must learn one more vital lesson: to disobey. The dog must learn to use its own judgment. If an obstacle is in the way, even when given the command to move forward, the dog must disobey. This shift of focus, from merely following instructions to being present and attentive to the outside environment, is what transforms a dog from trainee to valued service provider.

The same is true for you. I've given you many instructions on how to appear confident and credible. The true test of your communication prowess, however, is how you interact in the world. If you'd like to join the elite field of exceptional communicators, you'll have to shift your focus.

> *People who have enough inner obedience to take their focus off of themselves and give their full attention to their listeners distinguish themselves as truly exceptional communicators.*

Up until now, this book has been about *you* focusing on *you*. The instructions have been fairly straightforward—maintain a strong posture, use a strong voice, make strong eye contact, use expressive gestures, and eliminate derailers. If you follow these instructions, you are likely to come across as credible, confident, and comfortable.

But what if you want more? What if you'd like listeners to describe you with superlatives such as inspiring, compelling, persuasive, dynamic, or charismatic? What do you have to do to achieve this response? *You need to focus on your listeners.*

People who have enough inner obedience to take their focus off of themselves and give their full attention to their listeners distinguish themselves as truly exceptional communicators.

Chapters 1 through 5 covered the basics —the basic price of admission into the credibility club. This chapter provides you with elite status. This is how you differentiate yourself from the competition.

Why do these chapter 6 codes of conduct gain you so much advantage? The answer is: Because they are exceedingly difficult to master. First, you must get the basic skills solidly embedded into your subroutines. There's no way a guide dog can be effective if it's still struggling with the basic instructions of "sit" and "stay." Your basic skills must be reflexive, and that's the biggest hurdle most people face. Second, you can't fake these skills. Either you're focusing on your listener, or you're not. There's no pretending.

> ### Focus Codes of Conduct
> - **Project your energy: Meet your audience in their seats.**
> - **Elicit a response: Get their heads to nod.**
> - **Actively listen: Participate even when listening.**

Bedside manners

Many people work in industries where it's not just competence that matters. It's also the ability to connect sincerely with people on a human level. How often have you had an appointment with a physician who treated you like a list of symptoms? He was competent and professional, but you felt like just another patient chart on his rounds. Then again, perhaps you've been lucky enough to have the opposite experience during which a doctor seemed genuinely focused on you as an individual.

The difference in behavior can be subtle. What is the aloof doctor doing differently from the connected doctor? They both may have strong voices and strong postures. They both may look at you rather than the floor. The connected doctor, however, isn't just looking; he is *seeing*. And he's not just listening; he is *paying attention*. His focus is on *you* rather than on himself or his watch.

The codes in this chapter include the ability to project, to elicit a response, and to listen actively. Together they create a dynamic 360-degree communication loop that helps you make that vital connection.

FOCUS CODE #1
Project your energy: Meet your audience in their seats

Projection is a combination of things—optimal eye contact, volume, energy, and expression—working together to take your message all the way to your listener. It takes aim and intention to calibrate exactly how much effort is necessary in any given setting.

Imagine you and I are playing catch, but I consistently throw the ball just two feet short of reaching you. With each toss, you need extra effort to retrieve the ball. At some point, you'd find this tedious and search out something more interesting to do.

When we play catch, our brains unconsciously calculate the exact parabola and precise force needed to land the ball in the other person's grasp. The same process should happen in communication. Our brains calculate exactly how much volume, eye contact, energy, and expression we need to get our message to the audience. Yet many people "land" their message a few feet in front of the listener instead of hitting the target exactly. The most common communication mistake people make, no matter what their profession or organization, is failure to put enough effort into speaking. They simply don't throw the ball hard enough. Likewise, the biggest transformation I see is when they learn to recalibrate how much energy it really takes and begin to truly *land* their message.

Projection is more than just throwing the message harder, however. You need to aim. It takes the same amount of energy for me to throw the ball directly to you as it takes to throw it three degrees to the right. Any good pitching coach will tell you the first rule in *hitting* your target is *seeing* your target. To aim effectively, you first must fully see your listeners.

Projection is intentionally setting your skills at optimum. This requires continual adjustment, because optimal projection differs from one situation to another. Whether you are sitting across the desk from someone, talking on the phone, or standing at the front of an audience, imagine creating a communication bridge that leads directly from your location to theirs. First, place your focus on your target and then internally calibrate the exact level of volume, eye contact, energy, and expression to land the message perfectly.

Practice exercise: Pitch your message

Sometimes playing a game of catch can help you develop the skill of projection. Stand about 10 feet away from a partner. For a few rounds, throw the ball a foot or two shy of the catcher. Notice how much fun (or not) it is. After a couple minutes, start tossing the ball accurately. Gradually step farther and farther away from each other, taking notice of the level of effort it takes to land the ball on target.

Next, say short statements while you throw the ball. "Spring is my favorite season" or "I'd like to live in Paris." Again, notice how much effort it takes to land your message effectively. For the rest of the day, wherever you go, try to calibrate the optimal level of energy you need to land your message perfectly.

FOCUS CODE #2

Elicit a response: Get their heads to nod

After you throw your message all the way to your listeners, you need to entice them to engage in the listening process. Eliciting a response is how you get your listeners to come to you.

The listeners' limits

In *The Articulate Executive*, author Granville N. Toogood writes about the "18-minute learning wall." He describes how the U.S. Navy did a study in the 1970s to find out how long people can tolerate listening to other people talk. "The answer surprised a lot of people," Granville wrote. "The Navy found that in a classroom, presentation, or lecture environment, the audience's ability to focus on what the speaker is saying, then remember what was said, drops off at 18 minutes like the continental shelf plunging straight down into the abyss."

If communication is simply a one-way stream of information, people reach their limit in a short time. But the same people can have *conversations* for hours on end. In order to continually understand and retain information, the listener has to be an active participant. And making that happen is up to you, the speaker.

Elicit a response from your listener by creating opportunities in your script for them to participate. Ask questions, ask for their opinions, or ask them to paraphrase something you've said. Even saying their names or using rhetorical questions can keep your listeners more involved. The more you can get your listeners to reiterate your message, the more they will remember it.

Many people are very good at projecting but not as effective at eliciting a response. They may have learned how to throw the message—the drill sergeant approach—but not how to entice people to reciprocate. It's a one-way communication. Instead of being a game of catch, the exchange looks more like a game of dodgeball. But the purpose is not to hit the audience with the message; it's to throw it in such a way that they can catch it.

> *Even if your mouth is the only mouth moving, your nonverbal communication can have an ongoing dialogue throughout the communication.*

A powerful way to keep your listener engaged is through nonverbal communication. I call this "getting their heads to nod." When listeners nod, they aren't necessarily agreeing with you. Rather, they are saying "I'm listening" or "Go on . . . I'm with you."

Of course, some people nod, and some don't. There is a cultural component here. Personality also plays a role, and differences exist within organizations. The folks in the human resources department will typically nod more readily than those in the legal department. It's your job to ask for the head nod even if you don't actually receive one.

What signals can you give to elicit a head nod? Nodding yourself can do it, as can reaching out your hand in someone's direction. Just raising your eyebrows or changing your expression can do it: Any interactive communication signal might elicit one in return. When your body language talks to your audience, their body language just might talk back. Even if your mouth is the only mouth moving, your nonverbal communication can have an ongoing dialogue throughout the communication.

The unresponsive garage attendant

Outside my gym, I often encountered a garage attendant who treated me as if I were invisible. He greeted my hellos with a blank stare. Most people in this situation eventually stop saying "Hi" because it's uncomfortable to be consistently ignored. However, I decided to train him to see me.

I used the "kill him with kindness" approach. Every time I passed, I greeted him with a genuinely friendly "Hello!" I hoped he would eventually respond to my greeting and maybe someday even *initiate* one. I decided I would have accomplished my goal the day he said "Hi" to me first. I patiently persisted in this grand pursuit. It took about two months . . . but it finally happened. He now offers a friendly greeting every time I walk by.

- **Moral number one:** Communication is reciprocal.
  It just might take longer than you expect.

- **Moral number two:** Communication is reciprocal.
  Be careful not to let others dictate your communication skills.
  If I had stopped greeting the garage man when he didn't
  respond to me, he would have been the one training me.

Practice exercise: Tell stories at the dinner table

Ah, Thanksgiving dinner, reunions, and birthday parties. We set these times aside to visit with family and friends and to catch up on what's happening in each others' lives. These are also great times to practice your communication skills. When you're listening, you should be as attentive as possible. But when it's your turn to tell what you've been doing, keep your attention on those around you by actively trying to elicit a response. Anticipate this opportunity by choosing a story from your professional or personal life detailed enough to keep you talking for a couple of minutes. While you're speaking, do everything you can to get your listeners' heads to nod, as if they are saying, "Hmm, that's interesting. I'm listening."

What do you need to do? Start by really looking at them and then play up the interactive gestures: reach out, change your expressions, raise your eyebrows, and nod your head. In short, ask with your body language, "Is this coming across? Are you with me?" Secretly count how many times people nod back if you nod toward them.

As with so many skills in this book, if you raise the level of your communication, your listener will respond by being more involved. Don't wait for a special occasion to test this exercise. Try it tonight at dinner.

FOCUS CODE #3

Actively listen: Participate even when listening

Sometimes your credibility is won or lost not when you're speaking but when you're listening. Your listening image is just as important as your speaking image. Do you look tired and disconnected? Do you look respectful and engaged? Attentive listening requires you be an active partner in the communication regardless of whether you are speaking or listening.

George, one of my workshop clients, was having difficulties landing a job despite being an expert in his field. This was puzzling to me because he had excellent speaking skills at the front of the room.

I noticed, however, that when other participants took their turns speaking, George looked disengaged and bored. He didn't appear to be giving them the same level of attention or respect that they were offering him. It occurred to me that his problem finding a job might be his listening skills. If George had demonstrated these same behaviors in job interviews, potential employers would surely have been turned off.

When I shared my observations with George, he was stunned. He felt he indeed had given the other participants his full attention. He even reiterated for me the story the last speaker delivered. As often happens, how George *felt* was out of sync with how he *looked*. Looks count in listening.

Silence can speak volumes

It's not enough to pay attention; you have to look like you're paying attention. Active listening means demonstrating your attentiveness. Do this by keeping your posture energized: head up, body language open, navel pointing toward the speaker. When talking in a group, follow the conversation by keeping your eyes and nose aimed directly at whoever is talking. When appropriate, react to others' comments with nonverbal signals, such as a nod that implies "Yes, I'm listening." In one-on-one conversations,

> *Sometimes your credibility is won or lost not when you're speaking but when you're listening. Your listening image is just as important as your speaking image.*

you can also interject subtle verbal cues, such as "uh huh," "right," or "sure." If you're part of a team presentation, stay actively engaged even when your other team members have the floor. When one player has the ball in a basketball game, the rest of the team doesn't zone out to relax; they stay in the game ready to take the ball at any moment. Contribute when appropriate but keep your head up and your eyes on the speaker.

It's also important to know what your face looks like when you are relaxed. I have a dear friend who is one of the most positive, good-natured people I've ever met, but when she goes into listening mode and her face relaxes completely, she looks stern. She *feels* relaxed, but she *appears* judgmental. She is not blind to this fact, however. Because she's such an impeccable communicator, she knows she can't let herself relax completely, even when listening, or people might get the wrong impression. What level of communication customer service are you willing to offer to make sure people get the right impression of you?

The "true or false" quiz

I often use this "true or false" exercise in my workshops to help people develop the skill of attentive listening. Participants are divided into groups of four and seated at separate tables. Each participant must tell two stories about him or herself, one true and one false. Listeners must guess which story is true and which is made up.

After all the stories are shared, I tell them the real purpose of the exercise: to get them to pay attention to each other. When people take turns telling stories, they typically are not really listening to each other. Instead, when one person is talking, the listeners spend most of the time rehearsing in their heads the stories they plan to tell.

But when participants are tasked with telling fact from fiction, suddenly they focus on every word that's said. They notice every gesture and nuance. The lesson, of course, is to use this same level of attentiveness in all of your communication interactions.

Practice exercise: Take notes

At your next meeting, take notes about what you see and hear. Start by jotting down a quick assessment of the environment: the set-up of the chairs, the temperature, the lighting, and the décor. Then turn your focus to the people. Note each person's attire, mood, and level of involvement. Finally, focus on the content of the conversation. Keep a brief record of what everyone says. At the end of the meeting, notice if this level of attentiveness helped you to feel more present and engaged.

You might also try to reverse your perspective. Imagine one of your co-workers is taking notes about you. What behaviors are you displaying? Are your eyes on the action at all times? Is your posture open and energized? Do you look as if you are participating even when you're listening? When we imagine that others are watching us, we have a tendency to put our best image forward.

Take a field trip to the game store

Almost every town has one of those playful stores that carries unique board games and interactive toys. Visit this store and take the time to peruse the aisles and find something interesting to bring to your next gathering, whether it's an informal office party or a rainy day at home with the family. Look for something that will create lots of opportunity for conversation. Some of my favorites are Lifestories, Table Topics, or Chat Pack, where everyone takes turns responding to thought-provoking questions.

This gives you plenty of time to focus on all of the skills in this chapter. When it's your turn to speak, instead of focusing on yourself, see if you can pay attention to your listeners. Is your message reaching them? Can you invite them to respond nonverbally? When it's your turn to listen, actively demonstrate that they have your full attention.

When you put more intention into your communication, while playing a game or having a regular conversation, it's likely to be more enjoyable for you . . . and everyone else.

Moving on

We have covered a lot of behaviors that can win you credibility. Different situations, however, require different strategies. Does your job call for you to be a pillar of strength or a flexible team player? Is that potential client looking for a trusted authority or an amiable business partner? We all play different roles depending on the situation. By better understanding the balance between authority and approachability, you can accommodate all of your business interactions more effectively.

To watch a short video of the author
demonstrating the skills in this chapter,
scan the box above or
enter this URL into your browser.

www.thecredibilitycode.com/video/fegb27

CHAPTER 7

Authority Versus Approachability: Striking the Perfect Balance

"Sometimes it is not good enough to do your best; you have to do what's required."

– SIR WINSTON CHURCHILL

Everyone liked working with Victor. He was the epitome of a nice guy—friendly, cooperative, supportive, and positive. Because of his great attitude and long-term tenure with the company, he finally landed a managerial role. Unfortunately, those reporting directly to Victor wouldn't take him seriously or respond to him as a leader.

So Victor tried harder to be a good manager by becoming even friendlier and more accommodating. If his original message was "Please do this," his attempt to come on stronger sent the nonverbal equivalent of "*Pretty* please do this." Clearly this wasn't working: Victor needed to, metaphorically, grow a spine.

With a little bit of coaching, Victor began to cultivate his strength. He learned to stand up, speak up, and look his employees straight in the eyes. Soon, he was saying without apology, "I'd like this by five o'clock." Now when he speaks, people listen. He can even add "Please" without looking like a pushover. By adding more authority to his already approachable style, Victor garnered his colleagues' attention and respect.

> *Having the ability to shift your image to accommodate the situation will give you a great advantage.*

In our daily lives, we see a spectrum of communication styles that run from being authoritative to being approachable. Most jobs require a style balanced between these two qualities. A psychologist may need to be accessible and warm when interacting with trauma victims, but when giving a paper on the latest advances in neuroscience at a medical conference, she'll want to exhibit a more commanding style. An attorney may need to project an authoritative image in the courtroom, but when developing new client relationships at a networking dinner, he'll want to appear more amiable. Having the ability to shift your image to accommodate the situation will give you a great advantage.

If you exhibit a lot of authoritative behaviors, people are likely to view you as an expert—competent and capable. If you lean too heavily to that side, however, you might also come across as unreceptive, inflexible, or inaccessible. On the other hand, if your style leans toward being more approachable, you're likely to come across as personable and interactive. But if you tip that scale too far, you might seem lightweight, fluffy, or inconsequential.

The strongest communicators know how to be both authoritative and approachable *at the same time.*

The AvA Scale

In workshops, I help people assess where they fall on the Authority versus Approachability Scale or the "AvA Scale." I start by asking each participant to brainstorm the top three adjectives they hope others would use to describe them *in a perfect world.* If they choose words like *powerful, intelligent, trustworthy, influential, dependable,* or *honorable,* I know they'll need to bolster up their authoritative signals. If they choose adjectives such as *friendly, collaborative, dynamic, expressive,* or *charismatic,* however, they'll want to develop their approachable signals.

The list is almost always a combination of both sides—"smart, interactive, and dependable" or "personable, capable, and dynamic"—indicating that they're looking for a good balance between the two.

The problem is that many people want to demonstrate more authority or approachability but don't know how to do it. In their effort to push harder in one direction or the other they may even use behaviors that have a decidedly negative impact, inadvertently coming across as aggressive on the one side or extraneous on the other.

The good news is that the qualities of authority and approachability are not elusive. Very specific behaviors send one message or the other. Understanding the cues on either side can help you to bolster your image as needed.

All of the behaviors listed below have already been talked about in detail in the previous chapters. Now let's take a look at them in a slightly different context.

Try these behaviors if you'd like to appear more authoritative:

- Take up more space
- Maintain strong eye contact
- Stand or sit symmetrically
- Hold head still while speaking
- Use strong volume and resonance
- Use a downward inflection

To appear more authoritative, physically take up and command the space around you. That doesn't mean you wander around the room. It means you have a big bubble of energy around you. Your feet provide a wide base underneath you, your hands move freely in the space in front of you, and even the volume and vibration of your voice fills the air.

Maintain strong eye contact since the stronger your eye contact, the more authoritative you'll come across. This skill provides a double bonus: As long as your expression isn't locked into a poker face, strong eye contact will also raise your approachability.

Stand or sit symmetrically by keeping your spine tall and your shoulders level. If you picture authoritative icons, such as royalty, police officers, or military leaders, strong symmetrical posture is one of the first images to come to mind.

Keep your head still while speaking. This doesn't mean you shouldn't look around the room; rather it simply means you want to make sure that your head is not tilting and dipping like a bobblehead doll. You want to be "levelheaded" both literally and figuratively.

Use strong volume and resonance. The more power in your voice, the more personal power you appear to possess.

Use a downward inflection at the end of your phrases and sentences. A downward inflection says, "I mean what I say. You can count on this." The upward inflection sounds like a question mark at the end of your sentence. Speak in declarative statements and not questions.

Try these behaviors if you'd like to appear more approachable:

- Take up less space
- Use fluid gestures to reach out
- Use fluid facial expressions
- Use a wide range of vocal expression
- Elicit a response verbally and nonverbally

To come across as more approachable, physically take up less space. Commanding the space around you is a very good skill, but it's true that some people come on *too* strong—big movements, big energy, big voice. To look more accessible, they need to take up a little less space. Unless you consistently get feedback that you fall into this category, however, try one of the other methods to express approachability.

One excellent way to increase approachability is with fluid hand and facial gestures. *Literally reach out to people.* And keep your facial expressions in sync with your words. If your lips are moving, make sure your body language is also talking.

Use a wide range of vocal expressions by highlighting your meaning through stress, inflection, intonation, pace, and pausing. The more expression in your voice, the more the conversation sounds like it's for the listener's benefit.

Finally, elicit a response. This is perhaps the very best way to be approachable. Include your audience in the conversation, interact with them, and ask for their input. Or engage them nonverbally with your body language.

The lists of behaviors outlined above are not all inclusive. Many other behaviors can raise or lower your authority and approachability. Be cautious, however, because some behaviors can inadvertently undercut the positive aspects of your style. While having a poker face and a monotone voice may increase your authority, it won't help you forge a connection with your listeners, so I don't advise it. Likewise, bobbing your head and ending your phrases in upward inflections can increase your appearance of approachability but will significantly decrease your credibility.

All of the skills I've listed above are fairly safe: If you push the skill, you aren't likely to get pushback in another area. And my lists aren't mutually exclusive. With the exception of taking up more or less space (which you can fluidly move between), you can do both lists at the same time. In the long run, having a wide range of skills at your disposal will allow you to meet the needs of every situation.

Common misconceptions

When analyzing the qualities of authority and approachability, a couple of common misconceptions regularly come up. People often confuse being authoritative with being aggressive—as if they are the same thing. Likewise, people often confuse being approachable with being casual.

Authority without aggression

Demonstrating authority and being aggressive are very different behaviors. Consider this recent experience during a coaching session: I suggested a new client would benefit by showing a little more authority in her style. She responded, "Oh, no, no, no. I don't need to work on that! I get feedback all the time that I am way too authoritative."

> *It's important not to confuse authority and aggression because the two qualities often get the exact opposite result.*

I could immediately understand why she may have been told she was too authoritative, but she was misdiagnosed. She was actually coming across as too *aggressive*. She leaned forward as she spoke, punctuated her words with emphatic gestures, and held a strained smile on her face to hide her annoyance with my feedback. True authoritative signals look very different: a level head, relaxed gestures, and a direct gaze. It's important not to confuse authority and aggression because the two qualities often get the exact opposite result. The general population tends to respect people who are authoritative and resist people who are aggressive.

Casual versus approachable

People often associate being casual with being approachable. I once worked with a high-level executive who had gotten feedback that he was coming across as too rigid. So at his next town hall meeting, he played it very casual. He put his hands in his pockets and wandered nonchalantly about the stage. He kept his voice low-key and colloquial. But instead of appearing more approachable, he came across as aloof and unfocused.

Approachability doesn't come from a casual demeanor; it comes from being more interactive with your audience. This executive needed to put more energy into his style, not less energy. Coming dressed to his big meeting in sweatpants would have been more casual, true, but it wouldn't have made him more approachable. It's attentiveness to your audience that creates approachability.

When you lean too far

You may have received feedback in the past that you lean too far in one direction or the other. From the inside, it can be hard to identify what behaviors might be getting in your way. After leading thousands of on-camera coaching workshops, I've seen very consistent patterns emerge, and, to help you better self-assess, here are some commonalities I've noticed. Please keep in mind these are generalities; no one fits neatly into a box or stereotype. However, these may give you a starting place for evaluating what to address.

If the participant has been told he or she is perceived as too aggressive, stern, or unapproachable, the problem is often one or more of the following:

- Emphatic gesturing
- Lack of vocal expression
- Lack of facial animation (a poker face or locked-on fake smile)
- Inattentive listening skills
- Lack of eye contact

If the participant has been told he or she comes across as too light-weight or too "nice," the problem is often one or more of the following:

- Excessive head bobbing
- Weak posture (especially head tilted or chin down)
- Weak voice
- Excessive smiling
- Upward inflections at ends of statements
- Lack of eye contact

Practice exercise: Get an insider's view

Public figures who lean to the authoritative side include Dick Cheney, Donald Trump, Hillary Clinton, Carly Fiorina, Simon Cowell, Gloria Steinem, and Robert De Niro. Those who rely on an approachable style include Billy Crystal, Paula Abdul, Woody Allen, Michael Cera, Drew Barrymore, and Ellen DeGeneres. Most TV talk show hosts and national news anchors try to maintain a good balance between both sides.

Make a list of the people in your industry or organization who tend to be extreme in one direction or the other. Now list any exceptional individuals who display a wonderful balance between both sides. If these people are in your area, make an effort to get to know them. Take them to lunch and ask them to fill you in on their secrets to success.

Moving on

As the saying goes, "Knowledge is power." So far we've covered 25 specific codes of conduct that you can develop to help you appear credible, confident, and comfortable. Just knowing the impact of these skills may have helped you adjust some of your behaviors. But you may need a more detailed action plan for those negative habits that are too deeply ingrained.

In the next chapter, we'll take a deeper look at how to self-evaluate and create a course of action to keep your progress moving forward.

To watch a short video of the author
demonstrating the skills in this chapter,
scan the box above or
enter this URL into your browser.

www.thecredibilitycode.com/video/aukf49

CHAPTER 8

Self-evaluation:
Creating Your Action Plan

*"I hated every moment of training, but I said, 'Don't quit.
Suffer now and live the rest of your life as a champion.'"*

– MUHAMMAD ALI

An old native-American story begins with an elder talking to his tribe's youngsters. He tells them that they each have two wolves hiding inside—a vicious and competitive wolf and a kind and loving wolf. "The wolves inside you are constantly battling," the elder warns. One young man turns to the elder and asks, "But which one will win?" The elder answers, "Whichever one you feed."

The moral of this story is that your future is within your control. If you want any part of yourself to thrive, you must nourish and support it. Of course, that takes resources. For the busy professional, resources such as time and energy can be in short supply, creating a constant fight between the part of us striving to improve and the part content to remain the same. Your future depends on which you feed.

The myth about natural talent

People often ask me if the skills outlined in this book just come naturally to some people. The answer is, "Perhaps." Some people are more naturally gifted at sports or music, just as some people find it easier to have strong posture or use a strong voice. But natural ability is not as strong an indicator of success as is the willingness to practice. Great athletes and musicians don't reach the top of their fields without putting innumerable hours into perfecting their craft. Even with your average Joe, if he looks exceptionally athletic and trim, it's a safe bet he commits a good deal of time to exercising. It's a wonderful equation: If you spend time practicing any behavior, progress is *inevitable*. Hard work pays off whether you are naturally gifted or not.

When Renee first came to one of my workshops, she was fresh out of law school. Her movements were extremely stiff . . . *as if she didn't own her own arms and legs.* Her voice was meek, and she projected low status by consistently self-commenting.

> *Natural ability is not as strong an indicator of success as is the willingness to practice.*

However, Renee's dedication to self-improvement was extraordinary. For a couple of years, she took a workshop from me every six months or so. And every time I saw her, her progress was dramatic. Clearly, she had absorbed my feedback and steadfastly developed each area of weakness. I am not surprised that, over the course of a decade, she has become a senior partner in her firm and the president of her local bar association and has been listed in several publications as one of the top female attorneys in the country. Renee transformed herself from a timid, self-conscious person to a graceful, sophisticated, assertive leader. How? She committed to her own success and supported that commitment with many hours of practice.

Today, Renee often invites me to talk with her junior attorneys. She confesses to them, "Believe it or not, I started out as uncomfortable and awkward. But take heart, you, too, can transform if you invest the time."

The learning curve

Do you find it difficult to ride a bike? Your answer depends on whether you've ever taken the time to learn.

At first the process of learning to ride a bike takes all of your conscious attention. Your brain is completely preoccupied with the act of balancing, pedaling, steering, and keeping the darn thing upright. But after a short learning curve, your muscle memory begins to take over, and soon you're doing more cruising than falling. These behaviors then form a subroutine, and the task of operating a bicycle becomes effortless. Now your brain is free to multitask—you can watch the passing scenery, have a conversation, and even ponder deep philosophical questions, if you are so inclined. The bottom line is this: *Learning to ride a bike is hard; riding a bike is easy.*

The same is true for all of the skills in this book. One reason people find these behaviors difficult is that they don't persevere. They give up before the new subroutine is created. This is unfortunate because the learning curve is substantially shorter than most people imagine.

People in my workshops are amazed at how quickly they take on new skills. Most of the skills in this book are fairly straightforward: Keep your head level, hold eye contact for three to five seconds, speak up, and so on. With any one of these behaviors, practicing for a total of two hours will help you cement the skill into a subroutine—especially if you practice daily for short increments.

In workshops, I jump-start people. I don't expect anyone to become habitual in a one-day workshop. However, by the end of the day, they know what they need to work on and how to work on it. They have practiced enough in class to realize they are fully capable of mastering the skills—if they follow through.

This book can jump-start you. You've already taken a huge step in the right direction by reading this far. Sometimes just knowing more information can change a habit instantly. If you are shocked to discover your daily mocha frappuccino has more calories than a double-decker cheeseburger, you might suddenly and permanently end the habit of buying that drink. In regard to your communication habits, you've probably already committed to changing some of them simply because you now know more about how credibility is assessed. To truly transform your skills, however, it's best to put together an action plan.

The first step to any action plan is to pinpoint what to work on. You can learn that with a candid and fearless self-evaluation.

The importance of videotaping

Greta was part of a team of sales people who took my workshop on-site at her corporate office. When she stepped to the front of the room to introduce herself and describe her objectives, she said she felt very confident with her communication skills. "I'm a people person," she explained. "I enjoy interacting with customers and think I'm pretty good at it. I'm only here in this workshop because it's mandatory for my whole department. I don't think there's a lot I need to work on." Internally, Greta felt connected, engaged, and positive. In watching her video, she was stunned to see she had given her entire introduction *with her eyes closed!*

As I have said many times, what we feel from the inside can be very different from what the listener sees from the outside. If we are being ineffective, it is most certainly *unintentional.*

Have you had this experience? You are cruising through your day, and everything seems fine until you catch a glimpse of yourself in a window or mirror and discover something is definitely not right. Your collar is askew, there's ketchup on your shirt, or worse yet, what's that hanging from your nose! You wonder how long you've been walking around like that and ask yourself, "Was this visible during that meeting with my boss this morning?"

To truly verify if you have that proverbial piece of spinach in your teeth and get an objective view of yourself, you need an on-camera self-evaluation. Most people are reluctant to watch themselves on video because they believe they already "know" how they act, move, and speak. Yet the number-one comment I hear when people see themselves on video for the first time is, "Wow, I had no idea I was doing that."

A video camera is far more effective than watching yourself in a mirror. A mirror offers only a narrow, one-dimensional angle; a video camera can capture your full posture, gestures, eye contact, and vocal skills. So gather up your courage and arrange a video shoot.

In a perfect world, you'd capture a clip of yourself in action leading a staff meeting, giving a proposal, or making a formal presentation. If that's not possible, set up a video camera in your living room or your office. Give yourself an impromptu question or pretend to talk to friends or colleagues for a few minutes. You might try arranging the chairs with name tags to remind you to engage everyone "present."

Analyzing your video

Once you have a video clip, use the Self-evaluation Checklist (page 144) in appendix C to observe your behaviors. Watch the clip several times, looking at different behaviors each time. The image you project is a composite of all of your skills working together. But to gain a thorough diagnosis of your strengths and weaknesses, it's best to look at your skills individually. It's like sitting in a busy restaurant: You can selectively tune into the conversations at each table surrounding you, but you can't listen to all of them at once.

Start by watching your visual image—your posture, facial expressions, hand gestures, and eye contact. Try turning down the volume so you can isolate these physical behaviors. Next, listen to the vocal track. Turn your eyes away from the video to listen more intently. Finally, try running the video in fast-forward. If you have any physical patterns, like shifting back and forth or using a repetitive hand gesture, you are more likely to spot them in fast-forward.

Methodically work your way down the Self-evaluation Checklist. Note that some skills are very straightforward; you're either doing them or you're not. Posture, gesture, and derailers are in this category. However, some skills fall on a sliding scale from 1 to 5—voice and eye contact are in this category. You'll notice that the Self-evaluation Checklist doesn't include the Focus codes of conduct from chapter 6. This omission is intentional. For one thing, it's very difficult to rate these skills on camera. But more important, the focus codes of conduct are about your connection with your audience, and especially if you are doing this self-evaluation on your own, clearly you won't be able to assess that connection.

Qualities versus behaviors

Here's a vital tip about your self-evaluation: Be sure to identify the *behaviors* you need to work on rather than the *qualities*. For example, from your personal assessment, you may need to appear more confident. Take the time to identify the exact behaviors that are out of place. Is your head consistently tilted? Are your eyes darting around?

When it comes to implementing change, people often get lost because they try to adjust qualities rather than behaviors. It's somewhat vague to ask yourself to "show more confidence." It is fairly concrete, however, to tell yourself to keep your head level and hold eye contact for three to five seconds.

The entire purpose of this book is to break down these quality assessments into tangible, actionable steps. Every code of conduct in this book is defined as a behavior because behaviors are within your active control. Quality assessments are not.

Opening the door to colleagues and direct reports

To further enrich your self-evaluation, seek feedback from your friends, colleagues, and loved ones. Since unsolicited feedback is difficult to volunteer, it's best if you open the door yourself. Tell people you're working on your communication skills and you'd like to hear their observations. Keep in mind that those closest to you may also be blind to your bad habits (bless them!), or may not be able to articulate clearly what they have noticed. However, some colleagues may be waiting for the perfect opportunity to offer comments.

I recently coached the CEO of a design firm. When playing back his video, I pointed out that he consistently smacked his lips, clucked his tongue, and made a variety of nonverbal noises whenever he paused to gather his thoughts. He was surprised, embarrassed, and, most of all, angry. "Have I been doing this all along?" he asked. "Why didn't any of my staff bring this to my attention before now?" To me, the answer was obvious. I smiled and asked him, "What's in it for them?"

Unless you actively create a policy that supports candid feedback from all levels, your direct reports have nothing to gain and everything to lose by voluntarily pointing out your faults.

A note to all C-level executives: The higher up the corporate ladder you climb, the less likely you are to receive direct, honest feedback. Unless you actively create a policy that supports candid feedback from all levels, your direct reports have nothing to gain and everything to lose by voluntarily pointing out your faults.

Essential steps to creating your action plan

Using the Action Plan worksheet *(page 146)* in appendix D, follow along through the essentials steps.

Step 1—Self-evaluate: Videotape yourself speaking about a familiar subject. Use the Self-evaluation Checklist *(page 144)* from appendix C to identify what you're doing well and what you need to improve upon.

Step 2—Narrow it down: Select three skills as your highest priorities. Define them in terms of specific behaviors. You might begin by developing strong posture, strong volume, and strong eye contact. Those are the three pillars of effective communication.

> **Example:**
> Skill #1: Hold eye contact for three to five seconds
> Skill #2: Speak with optimal volume
> Skill #3: Stand in a balanced position

Step 3—Choose your exercises: Review the practice drills and field trips from the credibility codes that you want to work on. Select one or two exercises for each skill and feel free to modify them to better fit your situation or objectives.

> **Example:**
> Skill #1: Hold eye contact for three to five seconds
> Exercise: Place Post-it notes around the living room and practice talking through an upcoming proposal. Use sentence phrasing as a cue to move from note to note.
> Exercise: Practice at lunch in the cafeteria with co-workers. Focus on holding eye contact while discussing upcoming vacation plans.

Step 4—Commit to a specific time to practice: Clearly pinpointing a practice time increases the chances you'll follow through. Note the practice times in italics below:

> **Example:**
> Skill #1: Hold eye contact for three to five seconds
> Exercise: Place Post-it notes around the living room.

Practice talking through an upcoming proposal and use sentence phrasing as a cue to move from note to note.

Practice time: Tonight after dinner for at least 15 minutes.

Exercise: Practice at lunch in the cafeteria with co-workers. Focus on holding eye contact while discussing upcoming vacation plans.

Practice time: Tuesday, 12:30 p.m. lunch with Jon and Lauren

General practice strategies

Here are some helpful guidelines to make your practice sessions more productive:

Practice in low-risk environments: Develop your new skills in low-risk environments when mistakes won't threaten your credibility. Practice your skills around the dinner table with family or in the office with co-workers until such skills become habits. At this point, these good habits will follow you in the door for more important conversations.

Focus on one skill at a time: Trying to juggle multiple skills at the same time tends to degrade the quality of your attention. When practicing, give your full attention to one skill at a time. You don't have to master it before moving on to the next; feel free to alternate between skills until all of your skills have improved to optimal.

Practice often: The more frequently you focus on a behavior, the more likely it is to become a subroutine. For most skills, it's better to practice for short periods of time more often than to practice for long periods of time less frequently. As an example, when eliminating filler words, 5 minutes a day is more effective than 60 minutes at the end of the week. You will give a higher level of attention to each skill when practicing in shorter increments.

Find a partner: Even though this book is designed for self-study, most people advance more quickly when working with a partner. These skills are about communication, so teaming up is very helpful. And we are much more likely to keep to a practice schedule if we are reporting to another individual. Most important, a partner provides objective eyes and ears to remind you to focus and to offer feedback about your effectiveness.

Play games: Don't forget to play some of the games mentioned in earlier chapters. Play is an important learning tool in the animal kingdom; young animals learn the skills they need to survive by playing. They play because it's fun. Instead of seeing games as frivolous or superficial, see them as an entertaining way to learn new skills. I especially like board games that have a strong verbal component, such as Taboo or Balderdash, but try any game in which you have to communicate verbally to reach the objective. Pick any credibility code and focus on it while playing with friends or family. No one needs to know that you are working on your skills, and you'll have a safe environment in which to practice.

Choose a mantra: Focusing on several skills at once can sometimes cause your brain to go blank. Focusing on *one* behavior may keep you more centered and deliberate. Try using a mantra to unlock your best skills when it matters. Consider something very straightforward, like "volume" or "eye contact." Or it might be a little more metaphoric, like "get their heads to nod" or "meet them in their seats." Have a short but sweet focal point to help you get started in the right direction.

Practice with distractions: Once you have some proficiency with your skills, challenge yourself by adding a few distractions to your practice session. Test yourself in more public settings: Join a group like Toastmasters to give yourself a regular opportunity to practice in front of new faces. Volunteer to give a talk in your child's classroom or to make announcements at your church or networking organization. Take a class through a local continuing studies program and make a point to contribute your opinion often. Once you start to feel good about your new skills, feel free to test your limits in new ways.

Train your ideas to come when you call

Ruby, my nine-month-old puppy, was a star student in obedience training. In my living room, she can sit, stay, come, lie down, take it, leave it, and drop it on command. When I take her to the dog park, however, she gets so excited by the smells and other dogs that she seems to go completely deaf. She doesn't even know her name! My dog trainer tells me that Ruby doesn't own these skills until she is reliable in all circumstances. And if you've ever trained a dog, you know it's not a matter of whether the animal can perform the behavior; it's whether he or she will do so when distracted.

The same thing happens to humans. Sitting at our desks or in the comfort of our personal space, we are experts on our subject matter and can easily articulate the nuances of our field. But lead us to the boardroom or the podium, and we may fumble when composing a simple sentence.

It's easy to convince ourselves that we own our skills when we can perform them well under the best conditions. But then we berate ourselves if we underperform in situations when it really counts. Being at your best every time requires raising the bar on your own training. You need to be so comfortable, so habitual, that no distraction can pull you off your game.

But finding the time to practice is so inconvenient ...

You've heard the expression, "Practice makes perfect." I would amend this to "Intentional practice makes *almost* perfect." You create new habits by bringing your active attention to what you are doing.

Most people are resistant to practicing because their current behaviors require no effort. Changing any habit takes time and energy, and in our hurry-up-and-get-it-done world, these resources are in short supply.

Here's the secret: If you can create just enough momentum to move your skills through the learning curve, your new habits will become effortless. That's the beautiful payoff to practicing!

Unless you have a high-stakes job interview or a vital customer meeting coming up in the next couple of days, the penalty for not preparing your communication skills is not as immediately apparent. It's not like running out of gas on the freeway during rush hour. When your gas gauge is blinking, you know you must refill the tank no matter how late you'll be for that important meeting. The consequences are very motivating.

> *If you can create just enough momentum to move your skills through the learning curve, your new habits will become effortless. That's the beautiful payoff to practicing!*

Finding the time to work on your skills is tough. Everyone is too busy with too much to do, but that's the very reason people who do perfect their skills differentiate themselves from the pack. Everyone is in the same boat; the individual who takes the time to bring added value to his or her communication skills will stand out.

Practice exercise: What's in it for me?

Take a moment to brainstorm the answers to these questions: What will be the benefit to your life and career of developing your communications skills? What will you gain? And likewise, what are the consequences of not having your skills in peak condition? What will you miss out on?

If your answers to these questions are compelling, print them up and carry them around with you. The next time you feel you don't have time to practice, review what you've just written and practice!

The power of habits

In his book *Nobody Moved Your Cheese!*, Ross Shafer tells a story of exceptional customer service. Upon receiving a late-night cheeseburger from the hotel room service, he expressed disappointment that his soda was a diet Pepsi instead of the diet Coke he had ordered. The server apologized and explained that the kitchen was all out of diet Coke. Since Shafer was craving a diet Coke, he asked her to please take the Pepsi back.

Less than a minute later, the server returned with a cold diet Coke in hand. She had tracked down a nearby vending machine and purchased the soda with her own money. She refused to let Shafer reimburse her, saying, "I just want you to be happy at our hotel." Floored, Shafer went on a personal crusade to sing this woman's praises to her manager, the hotel manager, and the international headquarters of the hotel.

> *"Watch your thoughts; they become words. Watch your words; they become actions. Watch your actions; they become habits. Watch your habits; they become character. Watch your character; it becomes your destiny."*
>
> – Author unknown

When I first read this story, I was convinced of a couple of things: Clearly this woman was committed to customer service. But more important, her commitment to customer service was a habit. That was not the first time she had gone out of her way to help a customer; it was simply the way she did business.

After years of coaching business professionals at all levels, I'm convinced it's not ability that separates the top performers from the rest of the pack. It's habit. *Having* ability is very different from *developing* it. Cultivating your potential takes energy, discipline, perseverance, and a belief in yourself. It's *these* qualities that determine the top performers.

Shafer went on to say this young woman soon became the food and beverage manager, which is not surprising. Actions become habits, habits become character, and character becomes destiny.

Over the course of the book, I've outlined explicit actions you can take to build your appearance of credibility. It will take effort to develop these skills, but your willingness to invest this effort will differentiate you from the rest of the crowd.

To watch a short video of the author
demonstrating the skills in this chapter,
scan the box above or
enter this URL into your browser.

www.thecredibilitycode.com/video/acax22

Conclusion

Knowledge is a powerful ally in reaching your goals. Sometimes just having more information can change a habit in an instant. I rely heavily on video feedback because often, just by seeing themselves in action, people change their behaviors immediately and permanently. An outside perspective can be transformative.

Catching a glimpse of myself

One day when my kids were young, I spent the morning playing with them before taking them to the sitter's so I could run some errands. It surprised me that everyone I came into contact with greeted me with big, beaming smiles. It was like some magic dust had been sprinkled in the air. At the bank, the dry cleaners, and the grocery store, everyone seemed to be in a joyous mood. It was exhilarating until I happened to catch a glimpse of myself in the mirror at the coffee shop. I had forgotten that, when I was playing with the kids, I had drawn a kitty nose and whiskers on my face.

I had been walking around all day completely unaware of, literally, the nose on my face. Why hadn't anyone mentioned it? The answer, of course, is they thought I knew because a signal so blatant couldn't possibly be accidental.

This story contains three very important lessons:

- One, you can't expect you will receive outside feedback. People believe you are fully aware of the signals you're sending. And if you aren't aware, it might be uncomfortable to tell you. If you want honest feedback, you must actively seek it out.

- Two, the impact of our behaviors is cyclical. The reaction we get from one interaction contributes to the way we handle the next. By the time I got to the coffee shop, I was almost giddy with how strangely *they* were acting.

- And three, sometimes a choice we make at one point in our lives can linger with us even if we've forgotten we've made it. You must consistently self-evaluate to make sure the habits you developed at one time in your life are continuing to serve you.

Moving on . . .

Knowing the ground rules about how credibility is perceived is the first step. Having the courage to take a good look at yourself is the second step. The next and most vital step is to invest your time in developing these behaviors. Remember that when your skills become habits, they become effortless.

I hope this book has given you the tools and the inspiration to reach your full potential.

Sincerely,
Cara Hale Alter

*To watch a short video of the author
demonstrating the skills in this chapter,
scan the box above or
enter this URL into your browser.*

www.thecredibilitycode.com/video/chah48

I would enjoy hearing from you. Please feel free to contact me with questions, comments, or stories from your own experience by visiting thecredibilitycode.com.

Glossary

The AvA Scale: The scale that balances "authority" with "approachability"

Derailers: Unconscious communication signals that distract the listener from hearing the message, including excessive filler words or extraneous fidgeting

Diaphragm: The muscle located under the lungs that is responsible for volume and breath support

Emphatic gesturing: Punctuating one's words with sharp downward gestures with the hands or head

Fight-or-flight response: A primitive, automatic response that prepares the body to "fight" or "flee" from a perceived threat

Filler words: Words or sounds in speech that are superfluous and often used as placeholders to buy time while thinking. Examples include "uh," "um," "you know," "kind of," "sort of," "actually," "basically," "right," "I mean," "okay," and "like."

Friendship signals: Gestures that are intended to create a positive connection with the listener, such as smiling, nodding, raising the eyebrows, opening the eyes wider, changing expressions, and/or reaching toward the listener

Gesture box: The optimum airspace that hands should occupy while gesturing. Typically this airspace is no higher than the sternum, no lower than the hip joints, and no wider than the width of the shoulders.

Level four: The optimal level of communication. This level is as good as one can get without crossing the line and coming on too strong.

Masking: Locking the hands or face into a set position, restricting reflexive gestures or natural animation. This behavior, which is often an automatic-pilot response to feeling self-conscious, can be intentional or unintentional.

Meter problem: A conflict that arises when the internal perception of the speaker is out of sync with the external experience, as when a person believes she is speaking more loudly than she is actually speaking

Perception scale: The scale from one to five that evaluates how well an individual skill is being performed. 1–Absent; 2–Below average; 3–Adequate; 4–Optimal; 5–Too much

Self-commenting: Verbally or nonverbally commenting on one's perceived mistakes. This behavior can include apologizing for or flinching at minor trips of the tongue or audibly verbalizing one's internal criticism or negative self-talk.

"Sheep dog" technique: Method used to keep an audience engaged by consistently tending to all parts of the room. When using this technique, a presenter moves from one individual to the next, using a wide and random sweep, avoiding any observable pattern.

Subroutine: Any set of behaviors so habitual that they can be performed without conscious thought, such as reading, driving, or typing

Tail wagging: Any of a number of nonverbal behaviors that intend to send the signal of being nonthreatening. These behaviors may include asymmetrical posture, dipping chin, lowering volume, avoiding eye contact, rolling hands inwardly to show the underside of palms and forearms, shuffling feet, smiling shyly

Tend-and-befriend response: An automatic-pilot reaction under stress to "make friends with the enemy." The reaction usually involves lowering one's status by self-commenting, tail wagging, or sending friendship signals.

The T-rex: Posture characterized by pinning the elbows to one's sides while gesturing with hands close to the body

Tells (or poker tells): Any nonverbal signals that telegraph one's inner conversation

The Credibility Code
"Codes of Conduct"

Posture codes of conduct

- Keep your spine tall and strong
- Stand with your weight balanced equally over both feet
- Keep your head level
- Point your nose directly at the listener
- Command the space around you

Gesture codes of conduct

- Avoid "masking" your face and hands
- Engage your gestures from beginning of conversation
- Reach out to your listener
- Keep your hands in the gesture box

Vocal codes of conduct

- Speak with optimal volume
- Articulate clearly
- Keep your pacing relaxed
- Highlight your message with expression
- Engage your diaphragm for resonance

The Credibility Code
"Codes of Conduct"

Eye contact codes of conduct

- Hold eye contact for three to five seconds per person

- Engage everyone in the room

- Keep your focus up

- Be interactive

Derailer codes of conduct

- Eliminate fillers

- Avoid misplaced upward vocal inflections

- Avoid extraneous movement

- Eliminate self-commenting

Focus codes of conduct

- Project your energy: Meet your audience in their seats

- Elicit a response: Get their heads to nod

- Actively listen: Participate even when listening

A PDF of this worksheet is available at: www.thecredibilitycode.com/worksheets

The Credibility Code
Self-evaluation Checklist

	Yes	No
Posture		
• Spine is tall and strong	❏	❏
• Weight is balanced equally over both feet	❏	❏
• Head is level	❏	❏
• Nose is pointed directly at listener	❏	❏
• Head and arms move freely in space	❏	❏

	Yes	No
Gestures		
• Face and hands are relaxed (no "masking")	❏	❏
• Gestures are engaged from beginning of conversation	❏	❏
• Hands consistently reach out	❏	❏
• Gestures stay primarily within gesture box	❏	❏

	Yes	No
Derailers		
• Free of fillers	❏	❏
• Statements end in downward inflections	❏	❏
• Free of extraneous movement	❏	❏
• Free of "self-commenting" and apologies	❏	❏

	1 – Absent	2 – Below average	3 – Adequate	4 – Optimal	5 – Too much
Vocal Skills					
• Volume is full and consistent	☐	☐	☐	☐	☐
• Articulation is crisp and clear	☐	☐	☐	☐	☐
• Pacing is relaxed	☐	☐	☐	☐	☐
• Message is highlighted with expression	☐	☐	☐	☐	☐
• Vocal quality is supported and resonant	☐	☐	☐	☐	☐

	1 – Absent	2 – Below average	3 – Adequate	4 – Optimal	5 – Too much
Eye Contact					
• Contact is held for 3–5 seconds per person	☐	☐	☐	☐	☐
• Eyes engage everyone in the room	☐	☐	☐	☐	☐
• Focus is consistently up	☐	☐	☐	☐	☐
• Eyes, hands, and face interact with listener	☐	☐	☐	☐	☐

Comments:

A PDF of this worksheet is available at: www.thecredibilitycode.com/worksheets

The Credibility Code
Action Plan

Skill #1:

Exercise:

Time frame:

Exercise:

Time frame:

Skill #2:

Exercise:

Time frame:

Exercise:

Time frame:

Skill #3:

Exercise:

Time frame:

Exercise:

Time frame:

Notes:

A PDF of this worksheet is available at: www.thecredibilitycode.com/worksheets

Acknowledgments

First and foremost, I thank my dear husband and business partner, Ed Alter. Your keen insight and unique business perspective have contributed enormously to the content of this book. However, it is your devotion to my best interests, your willingness to take on more than your fair share of chores, and your ability to replenish me whenever I run low that made this book possible. Thank you. I owe this book to you.

Deepest thanks also to Roger S. Peterson. As my developmental editor and writing coach, you kept me on track every step along the way. Your guidance and good humor were invaluable.

Thanks to Leslie Waltzer for the interior layout design. You are a gifted designer and a kindhearted human being. Thanks to Andy Rado for the inventive cover design.

Thanks to my outstanding video production team, especially Lenny ("above and beyond") Levy, Darius Milne, and Carolyn Luu. Special thanks to Chris Scott of Makeup Gourmet for the use of his studio, his expert makeup, and his unwavering positive attitude.

Thanks to all who helped me to transform the manuscript from rough draft to polished product, especially Mariella Krause, Helen Chang, Amy Bauman, Debra Gates, and Deborah Taylor.

I'm indebted to many friends and colleagues who contributed their professional expertise to this project. Thanks to . . . Christine Carswell for reading an early draft and offering line-by-line comments . . .

Patricia Ryan Madson for reading my proposal and contributing superb constructive advice . . . Dianne Platner and Jeevan Sivasubramaniam for generously sharing their knowledge of the publishing industry and helping me choose the right path . . . Dan Roam for sharing his connections and encouragement . . . Robert Friedman for his fearless branding.

Thanks to all of my corporate clients. I sincerely appreciate your continued business over the years and have been touched by your enthusiastic support, especially Tom Bagwell, Kathy Reddick, David Haygood, Ida Abbott, Duncan MacMurdy, Steve Leech, Erin Constantine, Jessica Fitzgerald, and Joe Recchio.

Thanks to all of the participants who have taken my workshops over the last decade. I'm continually inspired, moved, challenged, educated, and enriched by the courageous individuals who seek feedback while the camera is rolling. Some of you have taken it upon yourselves to connect me with vital business opportunities. Your kind recommendations, given to the right people at the right time, have driven the success of my company. Thanks especially to Joan Haratani, Chad Barker, Jeannine Sano, James Barrese, Arvin Patel, Sabine Voegler, and Brenda Leadley.

Thanks to the enormously talented Rebecca Stockley and Lisa Rowland for being a part of the SpeechSkills training team. Your positive energy is infectious. Also, warmest thanks to Kirk Livingston who expertly handles the logistical details of our office.

Special thanks to Keith Johnstone, author of *Impro*, for first introducing me to the idea of status behaviors.

Thanks to the BATS Improv community for being a source of education and fun, especially William Hall, Carla Hatley, Barbara Scott, Regina Saisi, Diane Rachel, Kasey Klemm (who designed my very first website!), Ben Johnson, and John Remak. Thank you for brainstorming on my behalf.

Thanks to my personal friends who went out of their way to offer moral support, check on my progress, and contribute whenever possible, especially Amanda MacLean, Chris Curavo, Teresa Roberts, Rita Bell,

Tom Rusert, Darren Peterie, Janet Brehe Johnson, Shirzad Chamine, Jill and Jim Chriss, David Bangsberg, Lynn O'Kelley, Nan Crawford, and Matt Peavler.

Namaste to my yoga teachers for keeping me strong, centered, and connected during the long writing process, especially Pete ("from the heart") Guinossa, Mark ("you're in the right place") Morford, and Les ("be amused by the discomfort") Leventhal. Your reach is greater than you know.

A sincere and enduring thanks to my parents, Mom and Dick, Dad and Melva, and my in-laws, Ed Sr. and Eileen, for many years of unwavering love and support. Thanks also to the entire St. Louis clan (Hi, Cindy!) for cheering me on from a distance.

And finally, I offer my most heartfelt thanks to my children, Nick and Cassie. The best moments of my life have been with you. You continually exceed my expectations.

About the Author

 As the president of SpeechSkills, Cara Hale Alter has provided workshops in "Projecting Credibility and Confidence" to hundreds of companies throughout the United States and Europe. A popular instructor at Stanford Continuing Studies and UC Berkeley Extension, Alter has a masters of fine arts degree in theatre and has won national awards for public speaking. She lives in San Francisco with her husband and business partner, Ed Alter, and their two teenage children.